NES

Essential Components of Elementary Reading Instruction

SECRETS

Study Guide
Your Key to Exam Success

NES Test Review for the
National Evaluation Series Tests

Dear Future Exam Success Story:

First of all, **THANK YOU** for purchasing Mometrix study materials!

Second, congratulations! You are one of the few determined test-takers who are committed to doing whatever it takes to excel on your exam. **You have come to the right place.** We developed these study materials with one goal in mind: to deliver you the information you need in a format that's concise and easy to use.

In addition to optimizing your guide for the content of the test, we've outlined our recommended steps for breaking down the preparation process into small, attainable goals so you can make sure you stay on track.

We've also analyzed the entire test-taking process, identifying the most common pitfalls and showing how you can overcome them and be ready for any curveball the test throws you.

Standardized testing is one of the biggest obstacles on your road to success, which only increases the importance of doing well in the high-pressure, high-stakes environment of test day. Your results on this test could have a significant impact on your future, and this guide provides the information and practical advice to help you achieve your full potential on test day.

Your success is our success

We would love to hear from you! If you would like to share the story of your exam success or if you have any questions or comments in regard to our products, please contact us at **800-673-8175** or **support@mometrix.com**.

Thanks again for your business and we wish you continued success!

Sincerely,
The Mometrix Test Preparation Team

Need more help? Check out our flashcards at: http://MometrixFlashcards.com/NESINC

TABLE OF CONTENTS

Introduction

Thank you for purchasing this resource! You have made the choice to prepare yourself for a test that could have a huge impact on your future, and this guide is designed to help you be fully ready for test day. Obviously, it's important to have a solid understanding of the test material, but you also need to be prepared for the unique environment and stressors of the test, so that you can perform to the best of your abilities.

For this purpose, the first section that appears in this guide is the **Secret Keys**. We've devoted countless hours to meticulously researching what works and what doesn't, and we've boiled down our findings to the five most impactful steps you can take to improve your performance on the test. We start at the beginning with study planning and move through the preparation process, all the way to the testing strategies that will help you get the most out of what you know when you're finally sitting in front of the test.

We recommend that you start preparing for your test as far in advance as possible. However, if you've bought this guide as a last-minute study resource and only have a few days before your test, we recommend that you skip over the first two Secret Keys since they address a long-term study plan.

If you struggle with **test anxiety**, we strongly encourage you to check out our recommendations for how you can overcome it. Test anxiety is a formidable foe, but it can be beaten, and we want to make sure you have the tools you need to defeat it.

Secret Key #1 – Plan Big, Study Small

There's a lot riding on your performance. If you want to ace this test, you're going to need to keep your skills sharp and the material fresh in your mind. You need a plan that lets you review everything you need to know while still fitting in your schedule. We'll break this strategy down into three categories.

Information Organization

Start with the information you already have: the official test outline. From this, you can make a complete list of all the concepts you need to cover before the test. Organize these concepts into groups that can be studied together, and create a list of any related vocabulary you need to learn so you can brush up on any difficult terms. You'll want to keep this vocabulary list handy once you actually start studying since you may need to add to it along the way.

Time Management

Once you have your set of study concepts, decide how to spread them out over the time you have left before the test. Break your study plan into small, clear goals so you have a manageable task for each day and know exactly what you're doing. Then just focus on one small step at a time. When you manage your time this way, you don't need to spend hours at a time studying. Studying a small block of content for a short period each day helps you retain information better and avoid stressing over how much you have left to do. You can relax knowing that you have a plan to cover everything in time. In order for this strategy to be effective though, you have to start studying early and stick to your schedule. Avoid the exhaustion and futility that comes from last-minute cramming!

Study Environment

The environment you study in has a big impact on your learning. Studying in a coffee shop, while probably more enjoyable, is not likely to be as fruitful as studying in a quiet room. It's important to keep distractions to a minimum. You're only planning to study for a short block of time, so make the most of it. Don't pause to check your phone or get up to find a snack. It's also important to **avoid multitasking**. Research has consistently shown that multitasking will make your studying dramatically less effective. Your study area should also be comfortable and well-lit so you don't have the distraction of straining your eyes or sitting on an uncomfortable chair.

The time of day you study is also important. You want to be rested and alert. Don't wait until just before bedtime. Study when you'll be most likely to comprehend and remember. Even better, if you know what time of day your test will be, set that time aside for study. That way your brain will be used to working on that subject at that specific time and you'll have a better chance of recalling information.

Finally, it can be helpful to team up with others who are studying for the same test. Your actual studying should be done in as isolated an environment as possible, but the work of organizing the information and setting up the study plan can be divided up. In between study sessions, you can discuss with your teammates the concepts that you're all studying and quiz each other on the details. Just be sure that your teammates are as serious about the test as you are. If you find that your study time is being replaced with social time, you might need to find a new team.

Secret Key #2 – Make Your Studying Count

You're devoting a lot of time and effort to preparing for this test, so you want to be absolutely certain it will pay off. This means doing more than just reading the content and hoping you can remember it on test day. It's important to make every minute of study count. There are two main areas you can focus on to make your studying count:

Retention

It doesn't matter how much time you study if you can't remember the material. You need to make sure you are retaining the concepts. To check your retention of the information you're learning, try recalling it at later times with minimal prompting. Try carrying around flashcards and glance at one or two from time to time or ask a friend who's also studying for the test to quiz you.

To enhance your retention, look for ways to put the information into practice so that you can apply it rather than simply recalling it. If you're using the information in practical ways, it will be much easier to remember. Similarly, it helps to solidify a concept in your mind if you're not only reading it to yourself but also explaining it to someone else. Ask a friend to let you teach them about a concept you're a little shaky on (or speak aloud to an imaginary audience if necessary). As you try to summarize, define, give examples, and answer your friend's questions, you'll understand the concepts better and they will stay with you longer. Finally, step back for a big picture view and ask yourself how each piece of information fits with the whole subject. When you link the different concepts together and see them working together as a whole, it's easier to remember the individual components.

Finally, practice showing your work on any multi-step problems, even if you're just studying. Writing out each step you take to solve a problem will help solidify the process in your mind, and you'll be more likely to remember it during the test.

Modality

Modality simply refers to the means or method by which you study. Choosing a study modality that fits your own individual learning style is crucial. No two people learn best in exactly the same way, so it's important to know your strengths and use them to your advantage.

For example, if you learn best by visualization, focus on visualizing a concept in your mind and draw an image or a diagram. Try color-coding your notes, illustrating them, or creating symbols that will trigger your mind to recall a learned concept. If you learn best by hearing or discussing information, find a study partner who learns the same way or read aloud to yourself. Think about how to put the information in your own words. Imagine that you are giving a lecture on the topic and record yourself so you can listen to it later.

For any learning style, flashcards can be helpful. Organize the information so you can take advantage of spare moments to review. Underline key words or phrases. Use different colors for different categories. Mnemonic devices (such as creating a short list in which every item starts with the same letter) can also help with retention. Find what works best for you and use it to store the information in your mind most effectively and easily.

Secret Key #3 – Practice the Right Way

Your success on test day depends not only on how many hours you put into preparing, but also on whether you prepared the right way. It's good to check along the way to see if your studying is paying off. One of the most effective ways to do this is by taking practice tests to evaluate your progress. Practice tests are useful because they show exactly where you need to improve. Every time you take a practice test, pay special attention to these three groups of questions:

- The questions you got wrong
- The questions you had to guess on, even if you guessed right
- The questions you found difficult or slow to work through

This will show you exactly what your weak areas are, and where you need to devote more study time. Ask yourself why each of these questions gave you trouble. Was it because you didn't understand the material? Was it because you didn't remember the vocabulary? Do you need more repetitions on this type of question to build speed and confidence? Dig into those questions and figure out how you can strengthen your weak areas as you go back to review the material.

Additionally, many practice tests have a section explaining the answer choices. It can be tempting to read the explanation and think that you now have a good understanding of the concept. However, an explanation likely only covers part of the question's broader context. Even if the explanation makes sense, **go back and investigate** every concept related to the question until you're positive you have a thorough understanding.

As you go along, keep in mind that the practice test is just that: practice. Memorizing these questions and answers will not be very helpful on the actual test because it is unlikely to have any of the same exact questions. If you only know the right answers to the sample questions, you won't be prepared for the real thing. **Study the concepts** until you understand them fully, and then you'll be able to answer any question that shows up on the test.

It's important to wait on the practice tests until you're ready. If you take a test on your first day of study, you may be overwhelmed by the amount of material covered and how much you need to learn. Work up to it gradually.

On test day, you'll need to be prepared for answering questions, managing your time, and using the test-taking strategies you've learned. It's a lot to balance, like a mental marathon that will have a big impact on your future. Like training for a marathon, you'll need to start slowly and work your way up. When test day arrives, you'll be ready.

Start with the strategies you've read in the first two Secret Keys—plan your course and study in the way that works best for you. If you have time, consider using multiple study resources to get different approaches to the same concepts. It can be helpful to see difficult concepts from more than one angle. Then find a good source for practice tests. Many times, the test website will suggest potential study resources or provide sample tests.

Practice Test Strategy

When you're ready to start taking practice tests, follow this strategy:

Untimed and Open-Book Practice

Take the first test with no time constraints and with your notes and study guide handy. Take your time and focus on applying the strategies you've learned.

Timed and Open-Book Practice

Take the second practice test open-book as well, but set a timer and practice pacing yourself to finish in time.

Timed and Closed-Book Practice

Take any other practice tests as if it were test day. Set a timer and put away your study materials. Sit at a table or desk in a quiet room, imagine yourself at the testing center, and answer questions as quickly and accurately as possible.

Keep repeating timed and closed-book tests on a regular basis until you run out of practice tests or it's time for the actual test. Your mind will be ready for the schedule and stress of test day, and you'll be able to focus on recalling the material you've learned.

Secret Key #4 – Pace Yourself

Once you're fully prepared for the material on the test, your biggest challenge on test day will be managing your time. Just knowing that the clock is ticking can make you panic even if you have plenty of time left. Work on pacing yourself so you can build confidence against the time constraints of the exam. Pacing is a difficult skill to master, especially in a high-pressure environment, so **practice is vital**.

Set time expectations for your pace based on how much time is available. For example, if a section has 60 questions and the time limit is 30 minutes, you know you have to average 30 seconds or less per question in order to answer them all. Although 30 seconds is the hard limit, set 25 seconds per question as your goal, so you reserve extra time to spend on harder questions. When you budget extra time for the harder questions, you no longer have any reason to stress when those questions take longer to answer.

Don't let this time expectation distract you from working through the test at a calm, steady pace, but keep it in mind so you don't spend too much time on any one question. Recognize that taking extra time on one question you don't understand may keep you from answering two that you do understand later in the test. If your time limit for a question is up and you're still not sure of the answer, mark it and move on, and come back to it later if the time and the test format allow. If the testing format doesn't allow you to return to earlier questions, just make an educated guess; then put it out of your mind and move on.

On the easier questions, be careful not to rush. It may seem wise to hurry through them so you have more time for the challenging ones, but it's not worth missing one if you know the concept and just didn't take the time to read the question fully. Work efficiently but make sure you understand the question and have looked at all of the answer choices, since more than one may seem right at first.

Even if you're paying attention to the time, you may find yourself a little behind at some point. You should speed up to get back on track, but do so wisely. Don't panic; just take a few seconds less on each question until you're caught up. Don't guess without thinking, but do look through the answer choices and eliminate any you know are wrong. If you can get down to two choices, it is often worthwhile to guess from those. Once you've chosen an answer, move on and don't dwell on any that you skipped or had to hurry through. If a question was taking too long, chances are it was one of the harder ones, so you weren't as likely to get it right anyway.

On the other hand, if you find yourself getting ahead of schedule, it may be beneficial to slow down a little. The more quickly you work, the more likely you are to make a careless mistake that will affect your score. You've budgeted time for each question, so don't be afraid to spend that time. Practice an efficient but careful pace to get the most out of the time you have.

Secret Key #5 – Have a Plan for Guessing

When you're taking the test, you may find yourself stuck on a question. Some of the answer choices seem better than others, but you don't see the one answer choice that is obviously correct. What do you do?

The scenario described above is very common, yet most test takers have not effectively prepared for it. Developing and practicing a plan for guessing may be one of the single most effective uses of your time as you get ready for the exam.

In developing your plan for guessing, there are three questions to address:

- When should you start the guessing process?
- How should you narrow down the choices?
- Which answer should you choose?

When to Start the Guessing Process

Unless your plan for guessing is to select C every time (which, despite its merits, is not what we recommend), you need to leave yourself enough time to apply your answer elimination strategies. Since you have a limited amount of time for each question, that means that if you're going to give yourself the best shot at guessing correctly, you have to decide quickly whether or not you will guess.

Of course, the best-case scenario is that you don't have to guess at all, so first, see if you can answer the question based on your knowledge of the subject and basic reasoning skills. Focus on the key words in the question and try to jog your memory of related topics. Give yourself a chance to bring the knowledge to mind, but once you realize that you don't have (or you can't access) the knowledge you need to answer the question, it's time to start the guessing process.

It's almost always better to start the guessing process too early than too late. It only takes a few seconds to remember something and answer the question from knowledge. Carefully eliminating wrong answer choices takes longer. Plus, going through the process of eliminating answer choices can actually help jog your memory.

Summary: Start the guessing process as soon as you decide that you can't answer the question based on your knowledge.

How to Narrow Down the Choices

The next chapter in this book (**Test-Taking Strategies**) includes a wide range of strategies for how to approach questions and how to look for answer choices to eliminate. You will definitely want to read those carefully, practice them, and figure out which ones work best for you. Here though, we're going to address a mindset rather than a particular strategy.

Your chances of guessing an answer correctly depend on how many options you are choosing from.

How many choices you have	How likely you are to guess correctly
5	20%
4	25%
3	33%
2	50%
1	100%

You can see from this chart just how valuable it is to be able to eliminate incorrect answers and make an educated guess, but there are two things that many test takers do that cause them to miss out on the benefits of guessing:

- Accidentally eliminating the correct answer
- Selecting an answer based on an impression

We'll look at the first one here, and the second one in the next section.

To avoid accidentally eliminating the correct answer, we recommend a thought exercise called **the $5 challenge**. In this challenge, you only eliminate an answer choice from contention if you are willing to bet $5 on it being wrong. Why $5? Five dollars is a small but not insignificant amount of money. It's an amount you could afford to lose but wouldn't want to throw away. And while losing $5 once might not hurt too much, doing it twenty times will set you back $100. In the same way, each small decision you make—eliminating a choice here, guessing on a question there—won't by itself impact your score very much, but when you put them all together, they can make a big difference. By holding each answer choice elimination decision to a higher standard, you can reduce the risk of accidentally eliminating the correct answer.

The $5 challenge can also be applied in a positive sense: If you are willing to bet $5 that an answer choice *is* correct, go ahead and mark it as correct.

Summary: Only eliminate an answer choice if you are willing to bet $5 that it is wrong.

Which Answer to Choose

You're taking the test. You've run into a hard question and decided you'll have to guess. You've eliminated all the answer choices you're willing to bet $5 on. Now you have to pick an answer. Why do we even need to talk about this? Why can't you just pick whichever one you feel like when the time comes?

The answer to these questions is that if you don't come into the test with a plan, you'll rely on your impression to select an answer choice, and if you do that, you risk falling into a trap. The test writers know that everyone who takes their test will be guessing on some of the questions, so they intentionally write wrong answer choices to seem plausible. You still have to pick an answer though, and if the wrong answer choices are designed to look right, how can you ever be sure that you're not falling for their trap? The best solution we've found to this dilemma is to take the decision out of your hands entirely. Here is the process we recommend:

Once you've eliminated any choices that you are confident (willing to bet $5) are wrong, select the first remaining choice as your answer.

Whether you choose to select the first remaining choice, the second, or the last, the important thing is that you use some preselected standard. Using this approach guarantees that you will not be enticed into selecting an answer choice that looks right, because you are not basing your decision on how the answer choices look.

This is not meant to make you question your knowledge. Instead, it is to help you recognize the difference between your knowledge and your impressions. There's a huge difference between thinking an answer is right because of what you know, and thinking an answer is right because it looks or sounds like it should be right.

Summary: To ensure that your selection is appropriately random, make a predetermined selection from among all answer choices you have not eliminated.

Test-Taking Strategies

This section contains a list of test-taking strategies that you may find helpful as you work through the test. By taking what you know and applying logical thought, you can maximize your chances of answering any question correctly!

It is very important to realize that every question is different and every person is different: no single strategy will work on every question, and no single strategy will work for every person. That's why we've included all of them here, so you can try them out and determine which ones work best for different types of questions and which ones work best for you.

Question Strategies

Read Carefully

Read the question and answer choices carefully. Don't miss the question because you misread the terms. You have plenty of time to read each question thoroughly and make sure you understand what is being asked. Yet a happy medium must be attained, so don't waste too much time. You must read carefully, but efficiently.

Contextual Clues

Look for contextual clues. If the question includes a word you are not familiar with, look at the immediate context for some indication of what the word might mean. Contextual clues can often give you all the information you need to decipher the meaning of an unfamiliar word. Even if you can't determine the meaning, you may be able to narrow down the possibilities enough to make a solid guess at the answer to the question.

Prefixes

If you're having trouble with a word in the question or answer choices, try dissecting it. Take advantage of every clue that the word might include. Prefixes and suffixes can be a huge help. Usually they allow you to determine a basic meaning. Pre- means before, post- means after, pro - is positive, de- is negative. From prefixes and suffixes, you can get an idea of the general meaning of the word and try to put it into context.

Hedge Words

Watch out for critical hedge words, such as *likely, may, can, sometimes, often, almost, mostly, usually, generally, rarely,* and *sometimes*. Question writers insert these hedge phrases to cover every possibility. Often an answer choice will be wrong simply because it leaves no room for exception. Be on guard for answer choices that have definitive words such as *exactly* and *always*.

Switchback Words

Stay alert for *switchbacks*. These are the words and phrases frequently used to alert you to shifts in thought. The most common switchback words are *but, although,* and *however*. Others include *nevertheless, on the other hand, even though, while, in spite of, despite, regardless of*. Switchback words are important to catch because they can change the direction of the question or an answer choice.

Face Value

When in doubt, use common sense. Accept the situation in the problem at face value. Don't read too much into it. These problems will not require you to make wild assumptions. If you have to go beyond creativity and warp time or space in order to have an answer choice fit the question, then you should move on and consider the other answer choices. These are normal problems rooted in reality. The applicable relationship or explanation may not be readily apparent, but it is there for you to figure out. Use your common sense to interpret anything that isn't clear.

Answer Choice Strategies

Answer Selection

The most thorough way to pick an answer choice is to identify and eliminate wrong answers until only one is left, then confirm it is the correct answer. Sometimes an answer choice may immediately seem right, but be careful. The test writers will usually put more than one reasonable answer choice on each question, so take a second to read all of them and make sure that the other choices are not equally obvious. As long as you have time left, it is better to read every answer choice than to pick the first one that looks right without checking the others.

Answer Choice Families

An answer choice family consists of two (in rare cases, three) answer choices that are very similar in construction and cannot all be true at the same time. If you see two answer choices that are direct opposites or parallels, one of them is usually the correct answer. For instance, if one answer choice says that quantity x increases and another either says that quantity x decreases (opposite) or says that quantity y increases (parallel), then those answer choices would fall into the same family. An answer choice that doesn't match the construction of the answer choice family is more likely to be incorrect. Most questions will not have answer choice families, but when they do appear, you should be prepared to recognize them.

Eliminate Answers

Eliminate answer choices as soon as you realize they are wrong, but make sure you consider all possibilities. If you are eliminating answer choices and realize that the last one you are left with is also wrong, don't panic. Start over and consider each choice again. There may be something you missed the first time that you will realize on the second pass.

Avoid Fact Traps

Don't be distracted by an answer choice that is factually true but doesn't answer the question. You are looking for the choice that answers the question. Stay focused on what the question is asking for so you don't accidentally pick an answer that is true but incorrect. Always go back to the question and make sure the answer choice you've selected actually answers the question and is not merely a true statement.

Extreme Statements

In general, you should avoid answers that put forth extreme actions as standard practice or proclaim controversial ideas as established fact. An answer choice that states the "process should be used in certain situations, if..." is much more likely to be correct than one that states the "process should be discontinued completely." The first is a calm rational statement and doesn't even make a definitive, uncompromising stance, using a hedge word *if* to provide wiggle room, whereas the second choice is a radical idea and far more extreme.

Benchmark

As you read through the answer choices and you come across one that seems to answer the question well, mentally select that answer choice. This is not your final answer, but it's the one that will help you evaluate the other answer choices. The one that you selected is your benchmark or standard for judging each of the other answer choices. Every other answer choice must be compared to your benchmark. That choice is correct until proven otherwise by another answer choice beating it. If you find a better answer, then that one becomes your new benchmark. Once you've decided that no other choice answers the question as well as your benchmark, you have your final answer.

Predict the Answer

Before you even start looking at the answer choices, it is often best to try to predict the answer. When you come up with the answer on your own, it is easier to avoid distractions and traps because you will know exactly what to look for. The right answer choice is unlikely to be word-for-word what you came up with, but it should be a close match. Even if you are confident that you have the right answer, you should still take the time to read each option before moving on.

General Strategies

Tough Questions

If you are stumped on a problem or it appears too hard or too difficult, don't waste time. Move on! Remember though, if you can quickly check for obviously incorrect answer choices, your chances of guessing correctly are greatly improved. Before you completely give up, at least try to knock out a couple of possible answers. Eliminate what you can and then guess at the remaining answer choices before moving on.

Check Your Work

Since you will probably not know every term listed and the answer to every question, it is important that you get credit for the ones that you do know. Don't miss any questions through careless mistakes. If at all possible, try to take a second to look back over your answer selection and make sure you've selected the correct answer choice and haven't made a costly careless mistake (such as marking an answer choice that you didn't mean to mark). This quick double check should more than pay for itself in caught mistakes for the time it costs.

Pace Yourself

It's easy to be overwhelmed when you're looking at a page full of questions; your mind is confused and full of random thoughts, and the clock is ticking down faster than you would like. Calm down and maintain the pace that you have set for yourself. Especially as you get down to the last few minutes of the test, don't let the small numbers on the clock make you panic. As long as you are on track by monitoring your pace, you are guaranteed to have time for each question.

- 12 -

Don't Rush

It is very easy to make errors when you are in a hurry. Maintaining a fast pace in answering questions is pointless if it makes you miss questions that you would have gotten right otherwise. Test writers like to include distracting information and wrong answers that seem right. Taking a little extra time to avoid careless mistakes can make all the difference in your test score. Find a pace that allows you to be confident in the answers that you select.

Keep Moving

Panicking will not help you pass the test, so do your best to stay calm and keep moving. Taking deep breaths and going through the answer elimination steps you practiced can help to break through a stress barrier and keep your pace.

Final Notes

The combination of a solid foundation of content knowledge and the confidence that comes from practicing your plan for applying that knowledge is the key to maximizing your performance on test day. As your foundation of content knowledge is built up and strengthened, you'll find that the strategies included in this chapter become more and more effective in helping you quickly sift through the distractions and traps of the test to isolate the correct answer.

Now it's time to move on to the test content chapters of this book, but be sure to keep your goal in mind. As you read, think about how you will be able to apply this information on the test. If you've already seen sample questions for the test and you have an idea of the question format and style, try to come up with questions of your own that you can answer based on what you're reading. This will give you valuable practice applying your knowledge in the same ways you can expect to on test day.

Good luck and good studying!

Foundations of Reading and Alphabetic Language

Building Rapid Word Identification and Automaticity

Rapid word identification and automaticity refer to the quick, effortless, and accurate recognition of individual words when reading. Speed and accuracy are strong predictors of comprehension, so the ability to identify words automatically plays an important role in reading development.

When readers come to unfamiliar words in texts, they pause to use reading strategies. This includes applying phonics skills and using semantic and syntactic clues. Using these strategies takes time, which may cause the reader to slow down. Applying strategies to decode words also requires significant processing in working memory, which is limited. This diverts attention away from comprehending the text, and comprehension may be negatively affected. When readers develop the ability to accurately and automatically identify words, they free up space in working memory to use for comprehension. This shift often occurs around second and third grade.

It is also important to remember that rapid word identification and automaticity are necessary for fluency but not sufficient on their own. Fluency also involves reading with appropriate phrasing and intonation.

Using Instructional Strategies to Build Automatic Recognition of High-Frequency Sight Words

Readers need several opportunities to see words before they become automatically recognized. Therefore, providing opportunities for repeated exposure to high-frequency sight words is an important goal of reading instruction and should be included along with explicit phonics instruction.

Sight words are commonly introduced to students a few at a time. The most frequently used words, such as *a, you,* and *the,* are typically introduced first. Some reading programs coordinate sight word lists with weekly texts, ensuring that students will have frequent exposure to each set of words as they are introduced.

There are several types of activities that can be done to build sight word recognition. Going on word hunts to locate and circle sight words in texts is one activity. Sight words can be built using magnetic letters or spelled in the air with fingers or wands. Activities that require students to read, build, and write each word are also commonly used. Additionally, flash card drills can be incorporated into the school day.

Typical Progression of Phonological Awareness Skills

One of the earliest phonological awareness skills children develop is the ability to recognize rhyming words. After recognizing rhyming words heard in stories, songs, and poems, children begin to produce their own sets of rhyming words. Alliteration, or identifying and producing words with the same initial sounds, is another early phonological awareness skill.

Later, children develop awareness of syllables. This involves both the ability to blend syllables to form whole words and the ability to break whole words into syllables. The ability to blend and segment onsets and rimes is also developed. Onsets are composed of the initial consonants or consonant blends in syllables, whereas rimes consist of the vowels and remaining consonants that follow. For example, in the word star, /st/ is the onset, and /ar/ is the rime. Phonemic awareness is the most advanced phonological awareness skill, and it is usually developed after the others.

Relationship Between Phonological Awareness and Phonemic Awareness

Although they are often used interchangeably, phonological awareness and phonemic awareness are distinct terms. Phonological awareness is a broader term that refers to the ability to identify and manipulate sounds in spoken language. This can refer to identifying and manipulating sounds at the word, syllable, or phoneme level. Example activities include rhyming, alliteration, breaking words into syllables, dividing syllables into onsets and rimes, and blending and segmenting phonemes.

Phonemic awareness is one specific component of phonological awareness. It focuses on the ability to identify and manipulate sounds at the phoneme level only. Phonemes are the smallest units of speech, and phonemic awareness is therefore the most advanced component of phonological awareness. It usually develops after other phonological awareness skills.

In summary, phonemic awareness is one specific component of phonological awareness.

Phonemic Awareness Skills

One early phonemic awareness skill is phoneme isolation, which is the ability to identify specific phonemes in spoken words. This includes identifying beginning (initial), middle (medial), and ending (final) sounds. Another skill is phoneme identification, which involves identifying the common sound in a list of words that have either the same beginning, middle, or ending sound. In phoneme characterization, students are given a set of words in which all but one have the same beginning, middle, or ending phoneme, and they must identify the word that doesn't belong.

In blending, a more complex skill, students are given the phonemes that make up a word in isolation. They must then identify the whole word formed by putting the phonemes together. In segmentation, students are given a whole word, and they must identify the individual phonemes that make up the word. Phoneme deletion involves removing one phoneme from a word and identifying what new word was formed. Phoneme substitution involves changing one phoneme in a spoken word and identifying what new word was formed.

Activities Used to Teach Phoneme Blending and Segmentation

Children often benefit from a multisensory approach to phonemic blending and segmentation. Elkonin boxes are one tool that can be used. Elkonin boxes consist of a series of connected boxes on paper. Students listen to a word and slide a penny or other token into a box each time they hear a new sound. For example, while listening to the word *cat*, students would slide three pennies into the boxes.

Students can also be given strings of beads, and they can move one bead for every sound, or phoneme, they hear. They can slide the beads back together as they blend the sounds to form the whole words again. Rubber bands can be used in a similar manner. Students can say whole words with the rubber bands un-stretched and then slowly stretch the bands as they segment the sounds. They can then push the rubber bands back together again as they blend the sounds to form the whole words.

Phonics

Phonics refers to the relationship between letters and the sounds they make. After children learn to identify letter names, they learn that each letter makes a predictable sound. They later learn that groups of letters, such as consonant blends and digraphs, make predictable sounds as well. This understanding of letter-sound relationships is known as phonics.

Understanding the predictable relationship between letters and the sounds they make is important for the development of both decoding and encoding skills. When early readers come across unfamiliar words, they use knowledge of letter-sound relationships to decode the words as one common reading strategy. For early readers, this is especially helpful for unknown words that follow predictable spelling patterns, such as CVC words. When children are engaging in early writing activities, they use knowledge of letter-sound relationships to write words, which is known as encoding.

Phonemic Awareness Vs. Phonics

Phonemic awareness and phonics are commonly confused terms, but they are not the same. Phonemic awareness refers to identifying and manipulating phonemes in spoken language. Phonics refers to the relationship between letters and the sounds they make. A key question to ask when deciding if an activity is related to phonemic awareness or phonics is whether or not any letters are involved. If letters and their sounds are involved, the activity is related to phonics rather than phonemic awareness.

For example, asking students what sounds they hear in the word *cat* is a phonemic awareness activity because they are identifying sounds in a spoken word. However, asking students to decode the word *cat* when it is written in a text is a phonics activity because students must use their understanding of letter-sound relationships to successfully decode the word. Students are also using phonics skills if they write the word *cat* by identifying the sounds that they hear and writing the letters that make those sounds.

Fluency

Fluency is defined as reading accurately with the appropriate speed and intonation. Beginning readers typically have to stop and decode unknown words frequently, which affects both speed and intonation. Over time, as readers develop rapid word recognition, their reading speed increases. Appropriate intonation is also developed through frequent shared and guided reading experiences.

Relationship Between Fluency and Comprehension

Research has shown that reading fluency is one major predictor of reading comprehension. Non-fluent readers burden their working memories with decoding. Sentences are read in a fragmented way, making it difficult for the brain to organize and make sense of what was read. After expending the energy to decode difficult words, they may forget what they have previously read. Fluent readers are free to use working memory for comprehending the text. They read using smooth, continuous phrasing, making it easier for the brain to make sense of what has been read.

Using Semantic Cues to Figure out Unknown Words and Making Meaning from Texts

Readers use multiple cueing systems to figure out unknown words and make meaning from texts. When readers use semantic cues, they use prior knowledge from personal experiences along with meaning contained in the text and pictures to make sense of what they are reading. When they are stuck on unknown words, they consider what they already know about the topic or look to context clues or pictures for hints.

To encourage the use of semantic cues, students should be exposed to a wide range of texts and experiences to build prior knowledge and vocabulary. Teachers can conduct picture walks before students read new texts to activate prior knowledge and provide hints about the meaning. Students can be encouraged to make predictions before and during reading based on prior knowledge and text clues. Know, what, and learn (KWL) charts can be completed to help readers activate prior knowledge, and graphic organizers can be used to highlight text connections. Readers should also be encouraged to ask themselves if what they have read makes sense to encourage miscue recognition and self-correction.

Using Syntactic Cues to Figure out Unknown Words and Making Meaning from Texts

Readers use multiple cueing systems to figure out unknown words and make meaning from texts. When readers use syntactic cues, they use knowledge about correct oral language structures and the ways sentences are put together to decode and make meaning. For example, readers may use knowledge about subject-verb agreement and word order to decode new words and make meaning from sentences.

To encourage readers to use syntactic cues, teachers can model types of complex sentences. Sentences from familiar stories can be deconstructed, and students can be asked to put them back together again. Teachers can also provide sample sentences that each have one word covered and ask students to guess the missing words. Teachers can then ask students to explain how they figured out the missing words. Readers should also be encouraged to ask themselves if what they have read sounds right to encourage miscue recognition and self-correction.

Decoding Vs. Encoding

Decoding refers to the process of translating print to speech, which is done by translating graphemes into phonemes. Graphemes are letters or groups of letters that represent a single sound, and phonemes are the smallest units of sound in language. When a reader uses strategies to read the printed word *chair*, he or she is decoding the word.

Encoding refers to the process of translating sounds to print using knowledge of letter-sound relationships. This is done by translating phonemes to graphemes. When a writer uses knowledge of the sounds letters make to write the word *hop*, he or she is encoding the word.

Observing how a developing writer spells can be used to assess phonics knowledge. It can provide information about the writer's understanding of when to apply certain spelling patterns. By observing the writer's work over time, a teacher can determine which phonics strategies the writer has mastered and which are still developing. This information can be used to plan individualized phonics instruction. For example, if a writer frequently spells CVCe words without the e at the end, the teacher may focus on this spelling pattern during guided reading lessons with the student.

Instructional Strategies Used to Teach Decoding of Common Spelling Patterns

Blending is a common strategy to teach decoding of CVC words. Students say the sound represented by each letter in the word and then state the whole word they made. To increase fluency, students can be encouraged to increase the speed of blending over time. Once CVC words have been mastered and students are introduced to consonant blends and digraphs, they use the same blending process with CVCC words.

For CVVC and CVCe words that cannot be decoded using blending, students can be introduced to the sounds made by each spelling pattern. They can then build and explore word families that contain the same spelling pattern, changing the initial sounds to build new, related words. For example, after identifying the sound that /ake/ makes, students can build *rake*, *cake*, and *lake* using letter tiles or magnetic letters.

Instructional Strategies Used to Teach Decoding of Multisyllabic Words

Although decoding instruction typically tapers off around second grade, it is at this point that students begin reading texts with more complex, multisyllabic words. Therefore, it is important to teach specific strategies that readers can use to decode these types of words.

One strategy is to teach students to identify the different syllables present in a word. This can be done by clapping each syllable or saying the word while looking in a mirror and observing how many times the mouth opens. Students can then be taught to recognize common syllable spelling patterns and the sounds that they make. These common syllable spelling patterns include the following:

- closed syllables, which end in a consonant and usually have a short vowel sound (e.g., rabbit)
- open syllables, which end in a vowel and usually have a long vowel sound (e.g., bagel)
- r-controlled vowels (e.g., carpet)
- vowel digraph pairs (e.g., detain)
- vowel-consonant-silent-e syllables, which usually have a long vowel sound (e.g., athlete)
- consonant-le words, which are usually found at the end of a word (e.g., maple)

Readers can also be taught to look for known parts of words, such as known prefixes and suffixes.

Consonant Blends and Consonant Digraphs

A consonant blend is a group of two or three consonants that blend together to make a sound, but each individual letter sound is still heard. Examples include *bl*, *fr*, and *sw*. Blends are typically introduced after readers have learned to decode basic CVC words, and they are introduced in groups according to the second consonant they contain. Blends containing two consonants are usually introduced before blends containing three consonants. When introducing each blend, the teacher shows students how the sounds of each consonant are blended together to form the new sound. Common words containing the blend can be listed, and students can go on word hunts to find additional examples of words containing the blend. Students can also sort cards containing pictures of objects whose names are spelled with consonant blends.

A consonant digraph is a group of two consonants that form a new consonant sound when combined. Examples include *th*, *sh*, and *ch*. Digraphs are also typically introduced a few at a time, with beginning digraphs introduced before ending digraphs. Creating lists of example words, going on word hunts, and completing matching and sorting activities can also be used to teach digraphs.

R-Controlled Vowels

R-controlled vowels are vowels that appear before the letter r in a word. Words containing this spelling pattern are sometimes referred to as bossy-r words, because the letter r changes the sound of the vowel. The r-controlled vowel pairs are *ar*, *er*, *ir*, *or*, and *er*.

To teach decoding of words containing r-controlled vowels, teachers can model blending of simple words containing these spelling patterns, sliding their fingers along the words as they blend them. For each word, they can point out that the vowel and r together make one sound, and they can generate a list of other words containing the same letter pair and sound. Students can also be given word or picture cards to sort according to which r-controlled vowel sound they contain. Another strategy is to provide a picture of an object that contains an r-controlled vowel in its name. The word can be written below the picture, with the r-controlled vowel omitted. Students can be asked to provide the missing letters to complete the word.

Benefits of Explicit Phonics Instruction

Research has shown that early readers benefit from an explicit and systematic approach to phonics instruction. Developing readers who receive explicit and systematic phonics instruction at an early age often show increased ability to decode and spell, along with increased reading comprehension skills when older.

Explicit instruction means that phonics lessons are purposely planned to address specific skills rather than waiting until problems arise with decoding words while reading. For example, a teacher may plan to focus on a set of consonant blends during one week of reading instruction. Systematic instruction means that the lessons follow a carefully planned scope and sequence, with phonics lessons progressing from basic to advanced. Early phonics lessons for kindergarteners may focus on letter-sound relationships, whereas first grade students may focus on decoding different spelling patterns.

Explicit phonics instruction is only one component of a balanced literacy program, and time should be allocated to focus on other components as well.

Role of Phonological Awareness and Phonics Skills in Reading Development

English Language Learners

For English language learners (ELLs), research has shown that phonological awareness in a reader's first language is a strong predictor of his or her ability to learn to read in a second language. This is especially true when the native language is closely related to English. Whereas phonological awareness in the native language can be beneficial when learning English, it may lead to overgeneralization of rules of the native language. Continued language experiences in the native language along with language scaffolding can be beneficial to ELLs as they learn English.

Some ELLs may also speak native languages in which there is not a one-to-one correspondence between letters and phonemes. They may also speak languages that use the same alphabet as English but where the letters represent different sounds. It is important for teachers to understand ELLs' prior knowledge and consider this when planning appropriate phonics instruction.

Additionally, some English phonemes may not be used in other languages. Introducing English vocabulary words that contain these phonemes helps give these sounds a meaningful context. Using poems and songs with repetition and rhyme can also be helpful.

Struggling and Proficient Students

Research has shown that phonological awareness and phonics skills are important predictors of reading success. For struggling readers, daily phonological awareness and phonics practice are important. Explicit and systematic instruction should be tailored to the individual needs of each student and based upon observation and assessment data. Once a teacher has determined which skills the student needs to improve, instruction should be included regularly to target these skills until mastered. Ongoing reading assessments and flexible groupings can help assure that struggling readers' individual needs are consistently met.

Phonological awareness and phonics assessments are important for proficient readers as well. Some proficient readers have developed strong rapid word identification skills without mastering the underlying phonological awareness and phonics skills. When they get into older grade levels and more frequently encounter unfamiliar vocabulary, they have difficulty decoding the text. Assessment data can be used to identify specific skills to practice in small-group instruction with these proficient readers.

Role of Natural Exposure to Phonics in Early Reading Development

Like explicit phonics instruction, natural exposure to phonics also plays a role in early reading development. This exposure occurs when children are involved in natural reading experiences, and they come across words they are unable to decode. Phonics instruction is provided in the moment to address the unknown words.

This type of phonics instruction is known as implicit instruction. It differs from explicit instruction, which progresses from part (letter sounds) to whole (whole words). Implicit instruction progresses from whole (unknown words encountered in text) to part (breaking down the words in order to decode them).

Implicit phonics instruction has some benefits. Because it occurs during natural reading experiences, the phonics skills are taught in context rather than in isolation. Readers are motivated to learn the skills needed to decode the unknown words and continue reading. Teachers can allow time to address unknown words while reading aloud or listening to students reading independently. However, research has shown that it is still important to schedule time for explicit and systematic phonics instruction as well.

Strategies to Teach Letter Identification

Most reading programs introduce letters gradually. Some suggest introducing letters that have high value to learners first, such as the first letters of their names. Others focus on letters that play prominent roles in the books they are reading for the week, whereas others sequence letters by physical characteristics. In general, it is best to avoid teaching commonly confused letter pairs simultaneously, such as b and d.

To develop letter recognition, students can be given texts and instructed to circle certain letters. They can play alphabet bingo and cover specific letters when they are called. They can sing the alphabet song while pointing to each letter. Additionally, they can go on letter hunts, where they search the classroom or building to find examples of specific letters in environmental print. To practice recognizing capital and lowercase forms of letters, students can play memory and find matches consisting of both letter forms.

Strategies to Teach Letter Formation

To teach letter formation, students can be given letter stencils to trace with pencils. They can also be provided cutout letters made from different materials, such as felt and sandpaper, to trace with their fingers. Later, they can attempt to write letters independently on writing paper following the school's selected handwriting program guidelines.

To practice letter formation using a multisensory approach, students can write letters with shaving cream or fingerpaint. They can also write letters in containers filled with salt or sand. Wax craft sticks, modeling dough, and pipe cleaners can be used to construct letter models. Large-sized letters can also be drawn using sidewalk chalk, and students can hop along the letter shapes to trace them. They can also trace letter shapes in the air with their fingers or toy wands. Additionally, students can be given outlines of letters, which they can fill in with buttons, dried beans, or other common objects.

Strategies to Teach Letter-Sound Relationships

Once students understand that letters are combined to form words that convey meaning in print, they begin learning that each letter makes a predictable sound. This is known as the alphabetic principle. Although different reading programs introduce the letters and sounds in different orders, most introduce the letter-sound relationships gradually.

In some reading programs, each letter has a song, poem, or chant that incorporates repetition of the letter name and sound. In others, a letter character or visual is produced, which includes a hint about the sound it makes. The visual often includes a picture of a common object that starts with the letter. Students can also be encouraged to find objects beginning with the letter sound they are learning. Tactile activities, such as building letters out of wax craft sticks or writing them in shaving cream while repeating the names and sounds, are also commonly used. Bingo and other similar games that require matching letters to their sounds can also be used.

Concepts of Print That Collectively Form a Foundation for Early Reading Instruction

Concepts of print are the conventions used to convey meaning in printed text. Children begin developing an understanding of these concepts from an early age through shared reading experiences with others and interactions with printed materials.

Understanding concepts of print includes recognizing the front cover, back cover, and title of a book. It also includes recognizing that the print, rather than the pictures, carries the message. Additionally, it includes directionality concepts, such as knowing that you read from left to right and from the top of the page to the bottom, with a return sweep at the end of each line of text. One-to-one correspondence between written and spoken words is another concept of print. Letter concepts are also important, such as knowing that words are made up of individual letters, identifying letter names, and identifying both capital and lowercase letters. Identifying the names and purposes of common punctuation marks used to end sentences is also a key concept of print.

Strategies to Teach Print Awareness

Starting at an early age, caregivers and teachers can begin introducing children to concepts of print. While reading storybooks and big books aloud, they can model how to hold the books, where the front and back covers and titles are located, and where to begin reading. They can also model directionality by following the text with their fingers as they read, showing the left-to-right movement and return sweep. They can point out different text features, such as capital letters and punctuation marks, and discuss their purposes.

When students are interacting with texts independently, teachers can ask them questions regarding concepts of print. For example, they can instruct students to follow the text with their fingers and pause after encountering punctuation marks at the ends of sentences. Teachers can also point out text features in environmental print, such as hallway signs.

Relationship Between Reading and Writing Development

Reading and writing are interrelated and should be taught together. Students who read a lot tend to have stronger writing skills, and students who write a lot tend to have stronger reading comprehension skills.

When students frequently read varied types of texts, they learn how authors convey meaning differently through tone, language use, and sentence structure. They learn about different types of genres. They often use the texts as models and experiment with these elements in their own writing. Students also increase their vocabularies through reading, and they develop automatic recognition of high-frequency words. Students may then integrate the new vocabulary words into their own writing and remember how to spell words they have seen repeatedly in texts.

When students learn to write, they learn about and use different sentence and text structures. Awareness of these structures can help students recognize and make sense of them when encountered in other texts. Additionally, when students write about texts they have read, it facilitates additional analysis and comprehension. For example, writing about whether or not they would recommend books to others requires students to evaluate the texts and provide support for their reasoning.

Characteristics of Writers in the Preliterate Stage of Writing Development

The earliest stage of children's writing development is scribbling. Children begin scribbling at random places on the pages and do not proceed in any consistent direction. They typically hold writing utensils, such as pencils or crayons, with their fists. Scribbling helps children improve their fine motor skills and sets the stage for the understanding that writing carries meaning.

Over time, scribbling begins to follow a left-to-right directionality across the pages. Drawings may be included to help convey meaning.

Eventually, strings of pretend, letter-like symbols are used. They are sometimes mixed with numbers. Students are able to explain the meanings they are trying to convey through their writing. This phase demonstrates a beginning awareness of concepts of print. Spacing between words is not initially included but develops over time. There is no evidence of letter-sound relationships in the writing at this stage.

Characteristics of Writers in the Emergent Stage of Writing Development

In the emergent stage, writers begin to form letters correctly. Initially, they often write using all capital letters. They also begin to use their understandings of letter-sound relationships to write words. Some sounds are correctly represented in words, typically starting with the initial sounds.

In this stage, writers also begin spelling some words correctly. The first written words typically hold high personal meaning to students, such as their names and words like *mom* and *dad*. They may also write words found in environmental print, such as the names of popular restaurants frequently seen on signs. Some high-frequency sight words begin to be spelled correctly.

Students in the emergent stage write with left-to-right directionality and begin using spacing to separate words. They also begin to use common punctuation marks to split their writing into sentences, although this skill is still developing. Because it requires a lot of energy to encode words at this stage, writing pieces are typically short.

Characteristics of Writers in the Transitional Stage of Writing Development

In the transitional stage of writing development, students begin using a mixture of capital and lowercase letters appropriately. They also correctly use several different punctuation marks. Their writing includes a broader vocabulary than when they were in the emergent stage.

Transitional writers know how to automatically spell many high-frequency words, and they use multiple strategies to encode words they do not know how to spell. These strategies include considering letter-sound relationships to record the sounds they hear, considering known spelling patterns, and thinking of related, known words. Writing includes a mixture of conventionally spelled words and phonetically spelled words that are readable.

Because transitional writers are able to encode many words quickly, they have more available energy to focus on writing development. They focus more attention on developing story elements and including descriptive details. They write longer texts than they wrote in the emergent stage, and their writing includes a mixture of text structures and genres. Transitional writers also have the ability to reread and edit their work.

Characteristics of Writers in the Fluent Stage of Writing Development

Fluent writers spell most words correctly and use capitalization and punctuation marks conventionally throughout their writing. They are able to edit and evaluate their own writing and provide constructive feedback to others.

With the ability to spell most words quickly and automatically, fluent writers are able to focus more on writing craft, such as using descriptive language and developing story elements. Author's voice begins to develop. Writing may span several pages. Fluent writers consider their audiences and purposes for writing and consider them during the planning process. They use multiple strategies to plan their writing, such as brainstorming and using graphic organizers. They are able to write texts in a wide range of genres and select appropriate text structures to fit their purposes. Additionally, fluent writers are able to independently use tools like dictionaries and thesauri to improve their writing pieces.

Stages of the Writing Process

In the prewriting stage, writers brainstorm ideas, decide on topics, and plan the structure of their writing. This may include brainstorming, using webs or other graphic organizers to map out main ideas and details, and creating outlines. Writers consider who their audiences will be and what their purposes are for writing.

In the drafting stage, writers create their rough drafts. The focus of this stage is recording thoughts. Students are encouraged not to worry about spelling, grammar, and punctuation errors, which will be corrected later.

In the revising stage, writers consider if any portions of the writing lack clarity or if any parts should be added or removed. They examine word choice and consider if there are ways to make the writing more descriptive. They also seek feedback from others about ways the writing could be improved.

In the editing stage, writers carefully check their writing for spelling, capitalization, punctuation, and grammatical errors. They also ask others to edit their writing to ensure no errors are overlooked.

In the publishing stage, writers share their writing with others. This may involve creating illustrated books, reading aloud in authors' circles, putting on plays, or presenting in other ways.

Teaching Students the Writing Process

Modeling is an important strategy to help students become familiar with the writing process. Teachers can lead their classes in creating shared pieces of writing, going through each step as a group. Teachers can also share examples of their personal writing as they introduce each step of the process. Multiple examples that represent writing from various genres should be included to show students how the process can be applied to different types of writing.

Teachers can post charts outlining the steps of the writing process in their classrooms. Regular time should be set aside to work on writing, and at the beginning of each session, students can identify which steps of the writing process they will focus on that day. This will help them establish goals for each session and maintain focus.

Teachers should also schedule time for frequent conferring with students to provide feedback and ensure they are staying focused on the process. Additionally, teachers can provide opportunities for students to reflect on the process and the changes they have made to improve their writing.

Benefits of Conferring with Students During the Writing Process

There are several benefits of conferring with students during the writing process. When writers know they will be frequently meeting with teachers, it increases accountability for following the writing process. It also gives teachers opportunities to provide timely feedback to students and personalize instruction based on their individual needs.

It is important for teachers to model the conference process for students before beginning. Students should be aware of the purposes of the conferences and the expectations for their roles. Additionally, students should practice routines for what to do while their teachers are conferring with others. This modeling and practice will increase the likelihood that conferences can be conducted without interruptions.

There are multiple ways that conferences can be conducted, but they typically include students sharing the progress they have made since their last conferences and discussing any questions or concerns they have. Teachers usually pick a few points to focus on with each student, showing specific ways that improvements can be made using examples or mentor texts. Teachers should use the academic language of writing in their conferences. Additionally, conferences should be positive and motivating in nature to help students develop positive feelings about writing.

Helping Students Write Effectively for Different Audiences

As part of the prewriting process, writers should be encouraged to identify their intended audiences. Once they have identified their audiences, they should consider several factors. One factor is how much prior knowledge their audiences have about the topics. This will affect what level of background information and detail the writers should go into to meet the audience members' needs. For example, writers who are explaining how to use computer programs will focus on different program capabilities depending on whether the audience members are beginners or advanced users. Another factor to consider is what types of relationships the writers have to their audiences. This will affect the level of formality used in the writing. For example, a friendly letter to a classmate will be less formal than a letter written to a government representative.

Teachers should give students frequent opportunities to complete authentic writing activities for varied audiences rather than only submitting assignments for teacher evaluation. They can also provide opportunities for students to compare and contrast texts that are written about the same topics but written for different audiences.

Helping Students Effectively Write in Various Forms and Genres

Genre studies are one way to help students learn to effectively write in different genres. In genre studies, classes study one genre at a time, in detail, over the course of a few weeks. They read many different mentor texts in the genre and discuss common characteristics. Students can then be encouraged to complete their own writing activities within the genre, using the mentor texts as models.

A similar approach can be used to teach students to effectively write in different forms. For example, when learning to write friendly letters, students can explore many different examples. They can discuss common characteristics and use the examples as models when writing their own friendly letters.

Another strategy is to provide a mixture of strong and weak examples of a genre or writing form and ask students to evaluate their effectiveness. They can discuss which examples they think are the most effective and what characteristics these examples display that make them more successful. Similarly, they can discuss which features the weak examples contain or lack that make them less successful. They can then be encouraged to consider these findings during their own writing activities.

Developing Writing Skills

Developing effective writing skills requires a multifaceted approach. Like reading, writing should be interwoven through the school day and all content areas rather than taught in isolation. It requires a combination of explicit skills instruction and opportunities to freely explore and experiment with writing. Skills instruction should include a wide range of topics, including spelling, grammar, language use, text structures, and more.

It is important to help students develop positive attitudes about writing. Building a community of writers where students can freely collaborate, share, and solicit feedback can help students feel safe and supported in the writing process. Students need to be explicitly taught how to solicit feedback from classmates and how to provide constructive and respectful feedback to others.

Because reading and writing are interrelated, students also need frequent opportunities to both read and write texts of different genres and purposes. They need to compare and contrast different texts and evaluate both their own writing and the writing of others. They should also be explicitly taught how to participate in the five steps of the writing process, and they should receive frequent feedback on their writing. Feedback should provide specific suggestions for improvement in a positive and encouraging manner.

Helping Students Effectively Compose Written Texts

While teaching the writing process, teachers should help students understand that quality writing takes time. They can model their own writing processes and share stories about the writing processes of favorite authors. Writing stamina can be developed gradually in younger students, with writing workshop time increasing as the year goes on.

Although students need models of quality writing, they also benefit from seeing weak examples. Students can evaluate a range of writing samples and contrast their effectiveness. Comparing both strong and weak examples will help writers identify the characteristics of quality texts and consider them in their own writing.

Students should also be encouraged to engage in multiple rounds of revision. Revisions should be based on feedback from both peers and teachers as well as personal reflection. Students should also be explicitly taught how to consider feedback critically and decide which suggestions to implement and which to disregard.

Additionally, teachers should monitor students' writing through observations and conferences and plan mini-lessons based on the issues they notice. For writing that will be evaluated, rubrics should be given in advance. Students should be encouraged to consult the rubrics and self-evaluate their own writing at multiple stages throughout the process.

Assisting Students with the Revision Process

Revising is often a difficult part of the writing process as students may struggle to see how they can improve their own writing pieces. First, it is important that students understand that the focus of revision is on improving clarity, detail, word choice, and other features rather than on the spelling and mechanical issues they will address during editing.

Modeling is often an effective way to help students understand the revision process. Teachers can share their own writing pieces and ask students to identify areas that do not make sense or could be explained in better detail. For example, teachers may ask students to close their eyes and visualize while they read one portion of their writing pieces aloud. After asking students to share their visualizations, teachers may revise the writing to include more sensory details. Students can repeat the visualization process and note the differences. Teachers can also model writing sentences in multiple ways and ask which ways sound best. They may also help students identify descriptive words that can be used to replace commonly used words, such as replacing the word *nice* with *amiable*. These lists can be posted in classrooms for students to refer to when writing.

Stages of First Language Acquisition

Until about four to six months of age, babies are in the cooing stage. Babies in this stage commonly make vowel sounds, which represent their first attempts at oral language.

From about four to six months until one year of age, babies are in the babbling stage. At first, they commonly make repeated consonant-vowel sounds, such as *ma-ma*. Over time, their babbling begins to show the expressive patterns they hear in the language around them. They repeat sounds that others respond to and reinforce.

From about 12 to 24 months of age, children are in the one-word stage. In this stage, children begin referring to objects by consistent, one-word names. These words may be real or invented, and children begin to use language to convey meaning to others.

From ages two to three, most children enter the telegraphic stage, when they string together words to convey meaning. The words that convey the most meaning in sentences are often included, whereas articles, conjunctions, and other words are omitted.

After age three, most children enter the beginning oral fluency stage. They now use more complex sentences and begin using sentence structure and syntax appropriately. They use language for a variety of purposes.

Stages of Second Language Acquisition

In the preproduction stage, English language learners (ELLs) are listening and taking in the second language. Comprehension is minimal at this point. ELLs may not yet speak to others in the second language, and this stage is therefore sometimes referred to as the silent period. ELLs may communicate with gestures or single words.

In the early production stage, comprehension is still limited. ELLs begin responding using one- or two-word answers. Vocabulary in the second language begins to grow.

The speech emergence stage is marked by increased comprehension. ELLs begin speaking in longer sentences, but grammatical errors may be present. Vocabulary in the second language greatly increases.

In the intermediate proficiency stage, ELLs are able to comprehend much of what they hear. They begin speaking in more complex sentences that contain fewer grammatical errors. They are able to fluently communicate with others in the second language for a variety of purposes.

In the advanced fluency stage, ELLs understand academic vocabulary and need little support to participate actively in the classroom. Students in this stage speak with near-native English fluency.

Components of Oral Language Development

Phonological skills are one component of oral language development. These skills include the ability to recognize and manipulate sounds in spoken words. Rhyming and identifying syllables are examples of phonological skills.

Syntactic skills are another component. Syntactic skills include understanding grammatical rules and how to correctly arrange words in sentences. Children begin by using simple syntax, such as combining two words to express needs and wants. Over time, their sentence structure becomes more complex.

Oral language also includes a semantic component, which refers to the ability to understand the meanings of words, phrases, sentences, and longer texts. The semantic component is vital for comprehension.

Morphological skills are another component of oral language development. Morphological skills include understanding the meanings of word parts.

Finally, pragmatics refers to understanding the social rules of language. Examples of pragmatics include knowing how to adjust the formality of language depending on the audience and knowing how to respond in certain social situations.

Relationship Between Oral Language Development and Literacy Development

Most children learn to speak through immersion in language-rich environments, with no formal speech instruction necessary. Starting at birth, these early language interactions help set the stage for later literacy development. Early language play, such as sharing songs, nursery rhymes, and poems, assists young children with the development of phonological awareness skills. Strong phonological awareness skills are a strong predictor of future reading success. Hearing spoken language also helps children understand syntax and how sounds and words are combined to form meaning.

As children engage in frequent and varied oral language opportunities, they also increase their vocabularies. Opportunities to use both social and academic vocabulary during listening and speaking activities assists students with comprehending vocabulary words encountered in texts.

Oral language experiences also help readers understand that language can be used for a variety of purposes, such as meeting needs, social interaction, and persuading others. This assists with recognizing author's purpose. An understanding of cultural norms and nuances is also developed through oral language experiences.

Additionally, comprehension requires the ability to combine literal meanings of words with prior knowledge and world experiences. Oral language activities, such as following directions, can assist with this.

Promoting Oral Language Skills

When engaging in listening and speaking activities with students, it is recommended to use vocabulary words in context to promote comprehension later. Research has shown that identifying vocabulary words on flash cards and other similar types activities has little effect on later reading comprehension, whereas the ability to recognize and use words in context does.

Students should also have many opportunities to listen and speak for a variety of purposes to both peers and adults. Friendly conversations, academic discussions, formal presentations, and social interactions are all examples of different types of oral language activities. Varied activities will help students learn to change their language structures to fit the purposes of the interactions. Teachers can change their language structures throughout the school day. For example, they might chat informally with students about their interests during a morning meeting and switch to academic language when discussing a novel.

Additionally, students of all ages can benefit from reading and listening to a large variety of texts containing different types of sentence structure, language, and vocabulary. Young children can also benefit from word play and phonological awareness activities.

Developing Listening and Speaking Skills

Like reading and writing, listening and speaking activities should be incorporated throughout all content areas rather than taught in isolation. Students should be given multiple opportunities each day to listen and speak for a variety of purposes.

Students can listen to texts in audio form, listen to teachers read aloud, or participate in paired reading activities in all content areas. Before beginning, they can be given specific purposes for listening to focus their attention. They can participate in role-playing scenarios to model common social situations and conflict resolution. They can be given frequent opportunities to present their learning to others using a variety of formats. Audience members can be instructed to ask specific and relevant questions, and presenters can be instructed to provide well-supported and evidence-based answers. Additionally, collaborative, problem-based learning activities can be planned, requiring all students to have roles within their groups.

For English language learners (ELLs) and students who struggle with speaking, partially completed scripts and/or sentence stems can be provided. These tools can assist students with outlining thoughts and organizing sentence structure before speaking.

Creating Learning Environments Supportive of Cultural and Linguistic Differences

Classrooms should incorporate culturally and linguistically diverse materials, including those that represent the cultures of students. Reading materials, artwork, classroom labels, and posters are all examples of diverse materials that can be included. Students should also have opportunities to share items that are meaningful to them with other classmates.

Additionally, English language learners (ELLs) should not be punished for reluctance to participate in discussions. Instead, they should be offered support and scaffolding when needed. When ELLs are in the early stages of English language acquisition, teachers can also use simple sentence structures and provide visual clues to support students' comprehension.

Teachers should also work to create nonthreatening and supportive classroom environments by modeling accepting attitudes. They can model and explicitly teach how to compare and contrast different cultures respectfully. When studying historical and current events, teachers can help students explore the events from different perspectives and discuss how culture can affect people's experiences.

Teaching Students Nonverbal Communication Skills

Nonverbal communication, sometimes known as body language, includes gestures, facial expressions, and posture. Verbal and nonverbal communication work together to convey desired messages. If nonverbal communication is inappropriate for the audiences or purposes used, the meaning of the verbal communication may be lost or misconstrued. For example, a child may thank a grandparent for a gift. However, if the child has a disappointed look on his or her face while speaking, the grandparent may believe the child does not like the gift.

Additionally, certain types of nonverbal communication can be interpreted differently depending on culture. What is socially acceptable in one culture may be considered rude in another. Students should be aware of the messages their nonverbal communication sends to different audiences.

Teachers can engage students in discussions about what messages are sent by different types of nonverbal communication. They can role-play common scenarios and have other students evaluate the messages conveyed through both verbal and nonverbal communication. Students can also watch video clips of realistic situations, such as job interviews, and evaluate the nonverbal language of the participants. When giving presentations, teachers also provide checklists outlining expected nonverbal communication, such as eye contact with others and strong posture.

Role That Oral Language Plays in the Development of Critical Thinking Skills

Oral language leads to the development of other communication skills. Babies first listen to their caregivers and later say their first words before they learn to read and write. Through listening, children learn to evaluate the messages of others and make sense of newly learned information.

Through speaking, they learn to organize and communicate their thoughts to others. All of these skills assist with the development of critical thinking skills.

Teachers can ask students to explain their thinking to others. They can also explicitly teach students to defend their answers using support and evidence. Students can also be explicitly taught to use strategic questioning when interacting with classmates. Strategic questions require higher-level thinking to answer, and questions with yes-or-no answers should be limited. For example, students explaining the results of science experiments might be asked to evaluate their processes and explain what they might do differently in the future. Additionally, students can respond to high-level questions about texts during class discussions and literature circles. For example, they can be asked to evaluate the ways that authors use persuasive techniques.

Types of Language Disorders

Language delays and disorders can fall into three categories. Receptive disorders make it difficult for people to understand the messages communicated by others. Expressive disorders make it difficult for people to communicate their thoughts and ideas to others. Mixed receptive-expressive language disorders involve difficulties in both areas. These disorders can either be developmental or acquired. Acquired disorders are caused by injury or illness.

Within each of these categories, there are many different types of disorders. Apraxia, stuttering, and articulation disorders are some examples of expressive disorders. Students with expressive disorders may find it difficult to produce certain sounds, organize their thoughts into sentences, or use language appropriately in social situations. Therefore, classroom activities that require speaking and/or writing may be difficult. Students with receptive disorders may find it difficult to remember details or follow spoken directions. For example, they may not remember multistep directions that are given verbally for assignments.

Meeting the Needs of Students with Language Delays and Disorders

Although students with language delays and disorders often receive professional speech therapy, there are many strategies teachers can use to support these students within the classroom.

Teachers should model treating students with language disorders respectfully. They should not interrupt students with expressive disorders or attempt to finish their sentences. Instead, adequate wait time should be provided. Students can also be given advance notice of the questions they will be asked, allowing them time to formulate responses.

Students with receptive disorders who have difficulties processing or remembering speech may benefit from receiving information in multiple forms. When giving project directions, for example, teachers can provide written directions and explain them verbally. Multistep directions can be broken down into simple steps. Visuals can be used to help students comprehend vocabulary used in speech. Additionally, teachers can ensure that they have obtained students' attention before speaking, and they can monitor students for understanding.

For students who struggle with language pragmatics, role-playing activities can be used to practice appropriate responses for a variety of common social situations, such as asking for help or greeting people.

Relationship Between Understanding English Grammar/Usage and Comprehension

There is evidence that having a strong understanding of English grammar and usage assists with reading comprehension. When readers are able to untangle complex sentences in texts and understand how the components work together to form meaning, they are better able to comprehend what was read. When answering comprehension questions, they are better able to locate key information within complex sentences. They are also better able to incorporate complex sentence structure in their own writing to convey meaning.

Understanding English grammar and usage includes knowledge of parts of speech, the roles that they play, and how they are arranged in English sentences. It also includes knowledge of how simple sentences can be combined to form complex sentences. Readers with strong syntactic knowledge are able to self-monitor their reading and recognize when something does not sound right due to decoding errors. The ability to self-monitor and make corrections when needed is also important for comprehension.

Teaching English Grammar and Usage to Aid Comprehension

One strategy to teach English grammar and usage to aid comprehension is to break sentences apart and analyze their components. Depending on the ages and prior knowledge of the students, this may include sentence diagramming, dividing sentences into subjects and predicates, and splitting compound sentences into simple sentences. Students may also be asked to label sentence types, choosing from simple, compound, and complex sentences.

Another strategy is to combine words to form different types of sentences. Young readers may begin by combining only subjects and predicates to form the most basic types of sentences. As new parts of speech are learned, students can add additional words to form more complex sentences. Students can also be given word cards containing scrambled sentences. They can be asked to arrange the cards to form sentences, analyzing each attempt by asking if the sentences they have built sound right and make sense.

When given comprehension questions about texts, students can also highlight the parts of the sentences that contain the relevant information needed to respond.

Spoken vs. Written English

Although there is some formal, scripted speech, most spoken English is informal and conversational in nature. Speech often includes a mixture of fragments and complete sentences and may include interrupting and switching between speakers. Grammar in spoken English tends to be less strict, and there is more flexibility in word order. There may be differences in pronunciation, pacing, and intonation among speakers, and listeners must adjust to these differences to comprehend what was said. Speakers can gauge the understanding of listeners and rephrase or re-explain when necessary. Unlike written text, there is no formal record of what was said to review later unless notes were taken, or the speech was recorded. If speaking is part of an instructional lesson, listeners may benefit from being given overviews of the topics and guiding questions in advance to help focus their attention on key information.

On the other hand, written English allows for careful and deliberate organization. It is typically more formal and features more complex structures than spoken English. Word order is more rigid. Writers cannot gauge readers' understanding or reexplain if necessary, so meaning needs to be clear. Readers are able to review the text later to clarify information.

Role of Frequent and Varied Reading Experiences

Frequent and varied reading experiences allow readers to see diverse examples of how authors write. They can compare and contrast different writing styles and analyze how the audience, topic, and purpose of writing may affect formality and structure. For example, expository science texts will likely differ from graphic novels in formality. The science texts may also include more content-specific vocabulary words and use sentence patterns designed to present facts rather than resemble conversations. Additionally, readers can see vocabulary words and different parts of speech in context and observe how they work together to build meaning. They can also see the effects of different writers' word choices on the moods of the texts. Overall, frequent, and varied reading experiences help readers become more comfortable with language.

Being exposed to varied texts also provides students with models of sentence structure and writing styles to emulate in their own writing. Students often consider examples of familiar texts that fit certain genres or themes, called mentor texts, when they write their own. Being exposed to a variety of reading experiences gives students more examples to draw upon when they are writing.

Inductive vs. Deductive Methods of Teaching Grammar

In inductive teaching, students read and analyze texts that contain similarities. They look for patterns and identify grammar rules by themselves. For example, a teacher might give students several compound sentences that contain semicolons to join the two component sentences. Students might be asked to determine what the sentences have in common, leading them to identify and discuss the use of semicolons to join two simple sentences. Benefits include active participation by students to determine the grammar rules and use of critical thinking skills.

Deductive teaching is another method. In deductive teaching, students are explicitly told grammatical concepts and rules before being asked to apply them to their own reading and writing. For example, a teacher might present a lesson on using semicolons to create compound sentences and then ask students to look for examples of this rule during independent reading experiences. One benefit of this approach is that it can be quicker than inductive teaching. Some students may also be more accustomed to this teacher-centered type of approach.

Both methods of teaching grammar can be useful, and teachers often use a combination of both in their teaching.

Many teachers also use writing workshops to introduce grammar through mini-lessons and conferences with students. Using students' writing as informal assessment tools, teachers can determine which grammatical concepts and rules individual students need to practice.

Role of Grammar in Helping Ells with Comprehension

Understanding grammar can assist English language learners (ELLs) with reading comprehension. It helps them understand different types of sentences. Understanding punctuation marks and word order of different types of sentences helps ELLs determine if something is a statement, a command, or a question.

Additionally, understanding the functions of different parts of speech helps ELLs identify the parts of sentences that carry the most meaning. This helps focus their attention on the most important words in each sentence. Recognizing words and affixes that signal verb tense also helps ELLs determine when the action takes place. For example, an ELL might recognize that the verbs in a text end in -ed and realize that the story takes place in past tense.

Additionally, using syntactic clues is one important strategy readers use to make meaning from texts. To use syntactic clues, readers must have an understanding of what sounds right in English. When ELLs develop an understanding of English grammar and word order, they are better able to self-monitor their reading and determine if something sounds right. They are also better able to use context clues if they have an understanding of correct word order in English sentences.

Teaching Ells English Grammar and Usage

English language learners (ELLs) should be taught grammar and usage skills in realistic contexts rather than in isolation. It is also helpful to design grammar lessons around familiar topics and vocabulary so learners can focus on the grammar and usage concepts rather than trying to decipher the meaning.

Teachers should also frequently model correct grammar and sentence structure through listening, reading, and speaking activities. One strategy is to read texts that model a specific grammar rule and ask ELLs to listen for examples of its use or apply the rules in their own writing. They can also be encouraged to look for patterns in grammar and usage, such as -ed and -ing endings.

Teachers also need to carefully consider when and how to address grammatical and usage errors made by ELLs. Frequent and immediate corrections can cause frustration. However, if specific errors are not addressed over time, they may become fossilized and difficult to correct. One strategy is to note repeated errors and address them later in mini-lessons rather than at the time they are made. Teachers can also pick a small number of errors to focus on at any one time.

English Language Parts of Speech

The following are the eight parts of speech in the English language:

1. Nouns describe people, places, and things, for example, he ate a chocolate **cupcake**.
2. Verbs describe action or being; for example, the dog **chased** the squirrel around the yard.
3. Pronouns are words used in place of nouns, for example, **she** works in the office building downtown.
4. Adjectives describe nouns or pronouns. They usually describe which one, what kind, or how many of something, for example, the **yellow** house is located on the corner.
5. Adverbs describe verbs, adjectives, or other adverbs. They usually describe when, where, why, or how something happens, and they often end in -ly; for example, the fish swam **quickly** away from the shark.
6. Prepositions are words that relate nouns or pronouns to other words in the sentence; for example, the chef put the dough **in** the oven.
7. Conjunctions join words, phrases, or clauses; for example, the teacher **and** the principal attended the meeting.
8. Interjections show emotion in sentences; for example, **ouch**—I bumped my elbow.

When readers come to words whose meanings they do not know, knowing the parts of speech can help them determine the functions the words play in the sentences. This will make it easier to guess the meanings using context clues.

Teaching Students to Recognize Different Parts of Speech

Parts of speech are typically introduced one or a few at a time. Nouns and verbs are often introduced first because they can be used as the building blocks of basic sentences. If an inductive method is used, students may be given a group of sentences with the same parts of speech highlighted and asked to determine what the words have in common. If a deductive method is used, teachers might explicitly teach what each part of speech does and provide examples.

Minilessons can also be used. A mini-lesson on nouns, for example, might include listing nouns that fit into the categories of people, places, and things. It might also include finding examples of nouns in texts or sorting words according to whether or not they are nouns. Teachers can also use shared reading and writing activities as opportunities to discuss parts of speech in context.

Sentence diagrams are pictorial representations that show how parts of speech work together to form sentences. Although sentence diagramming can help some students visualize sentence structure, it can be frustrating and tedious for others. Therefore, it can be considered as one component of grammar instruction if it fits the needs of the learners.

Word Analysis and Fluency Development

Typical Progression of Reading Development

Readers typically progress through four stages of reading development. The first stage of reading development is known as emergent reading. It is the stage in which readers develop pre-reading behaviors and begin understanding concepts of print. The second stage is called early reading. Early readers begin to use a combination of reading strategies and cueing systems to decode and comprehend simple texts. The third stage is called transitional reading. Transitional readers use a wide range of reading strategies to support comprehension of more complex texts. Rapid word recognition combined with effective use of strategies allows readers to read at an increased pace. Fluent reading is the last stage of reading development. Fluent readers confidently read and comprehend a wide range of complex texts independently.

Students' individual differences and prior experiences can affect at what ages and rates they progress through the stages.

Characteristics of the Emergent Stage of Reading

Emergent reading skills are strong predictors of future reading success. In the emergent stage, readers display pre-reading behaviors. They begin interacting with texts without actually reading the words. They learn the concepts of print, such as learning how to correctly hold books and understanding that print holds meaning. They begin to identify capital and lowercase letters, and they understand the predictable relationships between letters and sounds. They also begin to understand that letters are combined to form words and words are combined to form sentences.

Readers in the emergent stage also develop oral language skills. This includes phonological awareness skills, such as rhyming and alliteration. They also develop phonemic awareness skills, including the ability to blend, segment, and manipulate phonemes within words.

Emergent readers also enjoy having others read to them. They respond to texts that are read aloud by making predictions, retelling events, and other activities. They also react to illustrations and use them to make sense of the texts.

Instructional Strategies Used in the Emergent Stage

Teachers should read aloud to students in the emergent stage often, choosing from a range of genres. When reading, teachers should model concepts of print and how to make predictions, retell story events, and other reading strategies. Concepts of print should also be explored in environmental print within the classrooms and the schools. Teachers should create print-rich environments containing several different types of texts for students to explore. Students should be given multiple opportunities to interact with different types of texts daily, both with others and independently.

Teachers should also plan explicit instruction on letter identification and letter-sound correspondence and give readers opportunities to practice recognizing and forming both capital and lowercase letters.

Additionally, teachers should plan classroom activities to build emergent readers' phonological awareness and phonemic awareness skills. This includes opportunities to practice rhyming, alliteration, onset and rime manipulation, and phoneme manipulation.

Characteristics of Texts Designed for Emergent Readers

Texts designed for emergent readers should have pictures or illustrations that strongly support the print. They should have a limited amount of text on each page and use repetitive words and phrases. They should include several high-frequency and easily decodable words, and the text should be placed in predictable places on each page. Simple sentence structure should be used.

Additionally, books for emergent readers should be focused on familiar objects and topics that will activate readers' prior knowledge. This assists readers with comprehension and making connections and allows them to focus on print concepts. The vocabulary should also be familiar. Print should be large and contain wide spaces between letters and lines of text.

Some emergent texts follow a pattern in which only the last word in each sentence changes. For example, each page of a text might say, "I like to ____." The missing word could be easily guessed based upon picture support.

Characteristics of the Early Reading Stage of Reading Development

In the early reading stage of development, readers increasingly use strategies to figure out unknown words and make meaning from texts. They use a combination of graphophonic, syntactic, and semantic cues. After guessing unknown words using one type of cueing system, they cross-check their guesses using other cueing systems. They begin to self-monitor their reading and self-correct if they realize that errors have been made. They expand their vocabularies and their automatic recognition of high-frequency words. They use picture clues, knowledge of letter-sound relationships, and repetition to decode unknown words in longer and more complex texts.

Early readers also continue developing comprehension strategies, such as predicting and summarizing. They use a combination of these comprehension strategies to make meaning from what they have read. They begin to read silently and no longer need to point to each word while reading.

Characteristics of Texts for Readers in the Early Reading Stage

Texts for early readers contain more print than those for emergent readers. They include longer sentences, more sentences per page, and more pages per book. The texts also contain more complex and varied sentence structure. There is less reliance on picture clues than in books for emergent readers, with the print carrying most of the meaning. More complex and content-specific vocabulary words are included. Multiple spelling patterns are used, requiring readers to use a combination of decoding strategies. There is less repetition, or longer and more complex phrases are repeated than those in emergent texts.

Texts for early readers also frequently focus on more complex story lines. Descriptive language is often included. The content of these books is still typically familiar to readers.

Readers in the early stage understand a variety of genres and purposes for reading. Therefore, texts for this stage are varied in genre and purpose.

Instructional Strategies Used with Readers in the Early Reading Stage

Students in the early reading stage are beginning to increase their reading rates and build fluency. Teachers can provide students with opportunities to frequently read and reread favorite books, which will help them build fluency. In addition to using picture clues, teachers can also model using a range of reading strategies that incorporate all cueing systems. They can prompt students to use these strategies in their own reading, asking them to check whether their guesses look right, sound right, and make sense.

Early readers still benefit from continued explicit and individualized phonics instruction. Activities that focus on advanced phonemic awareness skills, such as phoneme substitution, are also beneficial. Additionally, students benefit from instruction on complex vocabulary words and spelling patterns. Teachers can also provide students with frequent opportunities to read varied text types and genres that incorporate more sophisticated vocabulary words and sentence structures than emergent texts.

Characteristics of Readers in the Transitional Stage of Reading Development

Readers in the transitional stage of reading development are able to engage in sustained, quiet reading for extended periods of time. They are able to read and comprehend longer, more advanced texts and can automatically identify a large number of high-frequency words. They have knowledge of complex spelling patterns, which they use to independently decode most unknown words, including multisyllabic words. They are also continuing to increase their fluency and reading rates.

Transitional readers also utilize more strategies to assist with comprehension than early readers. They have an awareness of text structures and can gather and synthesize information from multiple text features, including print, graphs, charts, and sidebars. They rely more on the print than the pictures for meaning. They can identify story elements, such as characters, setting, problem, and solution. Additionally, they develop higher-level comprehension skills, such as making inferences and drawing conclusions.

Characteristics of Texts for Readers in the Transitional Reading Stage

Students in the transitional reading phase are able to read more difficult texts than early readers. This includes both fiction and nonfiction texts covering a wide range of genres. It also includes both beginning chapter books and challenging picture books. Nonfiction texts may utilize multiple text structures and include features like graphs, charts, photographs, sidebars, and more. The topics may be either familiar or unfamiliar to readers. Some challenging and unknown vocabulary words may be included along with many high-frequency words. Story elements may be described in detail, and descriptive words and phrases may be included. There are numerous chapter book series designed for transitional readers.

Books written for transitional readers may have several lines of text per page. Some pages may be composed entirely of text, as in chapter books. The books may have many pages. There are clearly defined spaces between lines of text.

Instructional Strategies Used with Readers in the Transitional Stage

Because transitional readers are beginning to read more complicated texts of different genres, it is helpful to teach about text structures. Understanding text structures and where to look for main ideas can assist transitional readers with comprehension. Teachers can also teach strategies to determine the meanings of unknown vocabulary words by analyzing word morphology. This includes recognizing and analyzing both affixes and roots.

Teachers can also plan several opportunities for students to build reading fluency by rereading texts for meaningful purposes. They can also model advanced analysis and comprehension strategies during shared reading experiences, such as making inferences and drawing conclusions.

- 38 -

They can provide students with tools like graphic organizers to assist with comprehension during independent reading. Additionally, they can encourage readers to support responses with text evidence.

Teachers can also assist transitional readers with selecting appropriately challenging texts for independent reading.

Characteristics of Readers in the Fluent Stage of Reading Development

Readers in the fluent stage of reading development read complex texts both quickly and accurately. They read with appropriate expression. They automatically recognize high-frequency words and efficiently use multiple strategies to determine unknown words they encounter. These strategies include using cueing systems, context clues, and substitutions.

Fluent readers are able to comprehend a wide range of complex fiction and nonfiction texts. They understand content-specific and technical vocabulary words or use strategies and tools to determine their meanings. They have a strong understanding of different types of text structures and know how to efficiently use text features to locate key information. They understand multiple purposes for reading and writing and are able to understand texts from multiple points of view. Additionally, fluent readers use high-level thinking skills to comprehend what they have read. They are able to evaluate texts and argue points using text evidence for support.

Characteristics of Texts for Readers in the Fluent Reading Stage

Texts for readers in the fluent reading stage are complex, varied, and sometimes abstract. Complex text structures are often used. For example, they may use flashbacks or weave back and forth while comparing and contrasting two things. Fictional texts for fluent readers contain highly developed plots and character development. They often use descriptive and figurative language. Additionally, these texts may have multiple themes or layers that require deep analysis. Content-specific and technical vocabulary words are commonly used. Topics may be either familiar or unfamiliar to readers.

Texts for fluent readers rely mostly on the print to convey meaning. Photos or illustrations are mainly included to convey important information that may be difficult to explain in print. For example, photographs of animals may be included in biology texts. Illustrations may be included in historical fiction texts where the settings or characters may be unfamiliar to readers.

Instructional Strategies Used with Readers in the Fluent Reading Stage

Readers in the fluent stage often read texts about new and unfamiliar topics. Therefore, teachers can instruct them to activate related prior knowledge that may assist them with making sense of the new texts. They can also model how to efficiently use research tools to learn more about unfamiliar topics.

Teachers can also model and encourage readers to use close reading techniques to deeply analyze texts. This process includes rereading texts multiple times to analyze different layers each time. It also includes evaluating, comparing and contrasting, making connections, and using other high-level comprehension strategies. Teachers can also encourage readers to analyze texts from multiple perspectives, using text evidence to support their responses.

Because readers in this stage will frequently encounter content-specific and technical vocabulary words, teachers can also continue to model word analysis skills, such as analyzing affixes and roots.

Types of Knowledge Commonly Used in Education

There are many types of knowledge commonly used in education. Social knowledge is one type. This is knowledge about social conventions passed down within members of a community. It includes conventions related to expected greetings, manners, and conversational behavior.

Procedural knowledge is another type of knowledge. It refers to the knowledge applied to carry out procedural tasks. An example is solving a complex math problem using a multistep algorithm.

Physical knowledge refers to knowledge learned by observing the features of something. When students discuss the physical properties of rock samples, they are using physical knowledge.

Domain knowledge refers to the knowledge and skills used by experts in a particular field. For example, a student explaining how she completed a division problem using the terms *dividend*, *divisor*, and *quotient* is using domain knowledge.

Empirical knowledge refers to knowledge obtained from scientific experimentation and data collection. Determining the boiling points of different liquids as part of a science experiment is an example of empirical knowledge.

Role of Literacy in the Development and Application of Different Types of Knowledge

Literacy plays a large role in the development and application of different types of knowledge in the classroom. Social knowledge is passed down through oral language and written texts. Students learn about social norms through the actions of characters in stories and through discussing texts with others. For example, children learn about solving conflict with friends by reading about characters who work through conflict. They also learn how to listen attentively and take turns through participation in literature circles.

When students read nonfiction procedural texts, they develop procedural knowledge that can be used to accomplish tasks. Procedural texts also provide models of text structures students can use when explaining procedures to others.

Reading texts containing academic language helps students develop and apply physical, domain, and empirical knowledge. Developing their academic vocabularies can assist students with expressing their observations and conclusions using academic language.

Academic Literacy

Academic literacy refers to the knowledge and skills necessary to communicate effectively in academic situations. It includes content-specific knowledge and vocabulary, such as mathematical terms. It also includes general knowledge and vocabulary used across all content areas, such as the terms *synthesize*, *summarize*, and *evaluate*. Additionally, it refers to the ability to communicate effectively in academic situations through reading, writing, listening, and speaking.

Academic literacy helps students flexibly adapt their use of reading strategies according to the types of text used and the purposes for reading. It helps them acquire content-specific vocabulary needed to comprehend academic texts and effectively communicate their learning using a variety of response types. It helps them summarize, evaluate, and make connections among content acquired from multiple sources and across content areas. Academic literacy also helps students effectively communicate and collaborate with others to construct meaning.

Academic Reading vs. Reading for Entertainment

Academic reading refers to thoughtfully reading and analyzing academic texts as part of content area studies. Readers usually have specific purposes in mind before beginning academic reading. For example, an entomology student may consult a field guide to correctly classify an insect found during a nature hike. Another student may read a social studies textbook to identify some major causes of the Revolutionary War for an essay assignment.

Reading for entertainment refers to reading for fun. A student may select a fictional book from a favorite series to read on a rainy day.

When completing academic reading, readers often pay special attention to text structures and features to efficiently locate needed information. They may skim or skip around in the texts. They may stop to look up the meanings of unfamiliar vocabulary words. They may also read more slowly or reread passages multiple times to make sense of unfamiliar content.

When reading for entertainment, proficient readers still self-monitor their comprehension, but they have more freedom about which text elements they wish to respond to and analyze. They may also read at a quicker pace and choose to reread favorite parts for fun.

Characteristics of Literacy-Rich, Content-Area Classrooms

Literacy-rich, content-area classrooms include frequent teacher modeling of academic behaviors. This includes teacher modeling of thinking aloud, use of reading and writing strategies, and incorporation of academic vocabulary into regular activities.

These classrooms also include daily reading, writing, listening, and speaking activities. Students are engaged in reading, writing, and discussing a range of different texts and media in both print in digital form. Depending on the content area, this may include lab reports, journal articles, maps, historical fiction, diaries, graphic organizers, narratives, and more.

Students in literacy-rich classrooms are also encouraged to make connections between different sources and content areas. For example, readers may make connections between a historical fiction text about the Dust Bowl and what they have learned in science about weather patterns.

Additionally, teachers in literacy-rich classrooms encourage the respectful sharing of information and ideas among classmates.

Components of Fluency

Rate is one component of fluency. Rate refers to reading speed. Proficient readers adjust their reading speed flexibly depending on their purposes for reading. For example, they may read scientific textbooks containing technical vocabulary more slowly than graphic novels they are reading for entertainment. Rate is important for comprehension. If readers read too slowly, they may forget what they have already read and lose the overall meanings of the texts. If readers read too quickly, important points may be overlooked.

Accuracy is another component of fluency. It refers to decoding words correctly without errors. Fluent readers automatically recognize many high-frequency words and use multiple strategies to decode unknown words. Accuracy is important because frequent errors may affect comprehension, especially if errors are made on words central to the texts' meanings.

Prosody is another component of fluency. It refers to reading expression, including phrasing and intonation. Prosody affects the ways texts are understood. For example, readers should pause appropriately at commas to emphasize certain phrases. Using the correct intonation associated with each punctuation mark also affects the tone of the texts.

Progression of Fluency Development in Readers

Early readers devote most of their mental energy to decoding words. In this stage of reading, the focus is on developing reading accuracy, which is one component of fluency. Early readers practice high-frequency words and learn strategies to decode words with simple spelling patterns. Rate and prosody play lesser roles but are still practiced with scaffolding.

In the transitional reading stage, readers automatically recognize many high-frequency words and more efficiently use strategies to decode unknown words. There is still a focus on accuracy as readers encounter more complex vocabulary and spelling patterns. However, transitional readers also increase their reading rates and begin to read independently with prosody. As readers gain confidence with familiar texts, their fluency increases.

By the time they reach the fluent stage, readers are able to flexibly adapt their reading rates based upon their purposes for reading. Automatic recognition of most words results in reading accuracy. Fluent readers read with prosody, and they appropriately match their expressions to the texts.

Developing Fluency in Early Readers

When teaching early readers, the main focus is on developing accuracy. This is done through activities to develop automatic recognition of high-frequency sight words and explicit phonics instruction that teaches strategies to decode words with common spelling patterns.

To assist early readers with developing speed and prosody, teachers can encourage repeated readings of favorite texts. As readers develop more confidence with the texts through these repeated readings, their reading rates will increase. Because readers already know how to decode the words in these familiar texts, they also have more energy available to focus on expression.

Teachers should also frequently model fluent reading. This includes reading with appropriate speed, phrasing, and intonation. Teachers can also model disfluent reading, such as reading texts without expression, and ask students to explain the effects it has on comprehension. Choral reading of shared texts can also assist students with developing fluency.

Maintaining Fluency in On-Level Readers

Like struggling readers, on-level readers can benefit from frequent teacher modeling of fluent reading, choral reading, and opportunities to reread familiar texts. Additionally, they can benefit from partner reading. Partner reading allows students to hear fluent reading modeled by classmates and reread texts repeatedly while receiving feedback. Students should first be taught procedures for how to listen attentively to their partners' reading and provide effective and encouraging feedback. Teachers should always be mindful of individual needs when pairing students.

Reader's theater is another strategy to assist on-level readers with fluency. In reader's theater, students read scripts from appropriately leveled texts to perform for classmates. Through rehearsing and performing, students have multiple opportunities to reread the scripts. They must also practice reading with appropriate expression for their characters and reading with appropriate speeds so they can be understood by their audiences. Additionally, reader's theater allows students in the audience to hear models of fluent reading. In reader's theater, the focus is on the reading, and few or no props are used.

Interventions to Use Assisting Readers Who Are Struggling with Fluency

Readers who are struggling with fluency can benefit from frequent modeling of fluent reading. As teachers reread familiar texts, students can join in and read chorally, matching their phrasing, speed, and expression to the teachers' reading. Students can also listen to audio recordings of texts.

Readers who struggle with fluency can also benefit from repeated readings of texts. After initial readings, teachers can give feedback to students and help them set goals for rereading. For example, they may encourage readers to pause at the periods between sentences. It is important that readers are given passages within their instructional reading levels. Reading texts far below their instructional levels will not challenge the readers. Reading texts that are too difficult will result in readers stopping frequently to decode unknown words, interrupting fluency, and causing frustration. Encouraging repeated readings of texts with rhyming and repetition, including poetry, can also assist readers who are struggling with fluency.

Although teachers may monitor students' reading fluency over time, it is also important to create encouraging environments for readers. Continuously timing readers or forcing disfluent readers to read aloud in front of others may have negative effects.

Vocabulary and Comprehension Development

Encouraging Vocabulary Acquisition Through Reading and Writing Activities

If a new text contains unfamiliar vocabulary words that are central to the meaning and/or may be difficult to decode, a teacher may preview the words with the group. After introducing the topic of the text, the teacher may flip to the words, show students their spellings, and ask students to share what the words may mean based on prior knowledge and picture clues. Exposure to these words before reading will build readers' confidence and help them recognize and decode the words faster, maintaining fluency. Knowing the meanings in advance will also assist with comprehension.

When reading aloud to students, teachers may pause at new vocabulary words and model how to use context clues, prior knowledge, and picture support to decode and comprehend the new words. Students can be encouraged to use these strategies when reading independently.

Readers need repeated exposure to vocabulary words to develop automatic recognition and comprehension. Teachers may display classroom charts containing vocabulary words and their meanings, possibly using picture clues for young readers.

Students can also be encouraged to incorporate vocabulary words in their own writing. Word walls or charts containing the words can assist students with spelling and remembering the words' meanings.

Helping Readers Recognize and Explore the Meanings of Unknown Vocabulary Words

First, it is important for students to identify unknown vocabulary words when reading. Readers who are not monitoring their own comprehension may decode the words and continue reading, even if they do not understand their meanings. Teachers can model how to stop when they reach words they don't understand, even if they can decode them, and encourage students to do the same.

Next, readers need to determine which unknown words are central to the meanings of the text and worth exploring further. This is important because there may be many unknown words, and if readers stop extensively at each one, fluency and comprehension may be interrupted. Therefore, students can be encouraged to consider whether or not they can comprehend the sentences and overall meanings of the texts without devoting more energy to these particular unknown words.

If readers determine that the unknown words are central to the meaning of the text, they can be encouraged to use strategies such as using context clues, looking for known roots or affixes, or consulting dictionaries. Overall, readers should be encouraged to self-monitor their own reading and comprehension and determine when to apply known strategies.

Supporting Vocabulary Acquisition and Use Through Listening and Speaking

Young children begin their vocabulary development through listening well before they begin to read and write. Through listening to family members, caregivers, and others, children develop their meaning (oral) vocabularies. These are words that children understand when heard and eventually use in their own speech. These vocabularies can be developed by talking to children frequently for a variety of purposes, reading to them, exposing them to songs, rhymes, and poems, and many other language activities.

- 44 -

Children continue to build vocabulary through listening and speaking activities when they begin school. Teachers can read aloud to students often, varying the genres and purposes for listening. Engaging students in discussions about what was read aloud can give students a purpose for listening and opportunities to use text-related vocabulary in their own oral responses. Teachers can also incorporate key vocabulary words in class discussions.

Students should also have frequent opportunities to speak in the classroom. In addition to informal class discussions, students can present projects to classmates and explain their thinking during problem-solving. They can be encouraged to use content-specific vocabulary when appropriate.

Homographs

Homographs are words that are spelled the same but may be pronounced differently and have different meanings. An example of a homograph pair is bat (baseball bat) and bat (the flying mammal).

After explaining the meaning of homographs, teachers can assist students with generating lists of homograph pairs. Teachers can provide sentences using homographs, and students can identify them and their meanings. Students can also look for homographs in texts and play matching games to find cards with two different definitions for the same word.

Homographs have different meanings, so it is important for readers to be able to identify which meanings are being used when they encounter homographs in texts. Readers can be encouraged to use context clues to assist with determining the meanings. Readers can also be encouraged to self-monitor their understanding of each homograph's meaning by asking themselves if what they have read makes sense. Because homograph pairs can also be pronounced differently, readers can be encouraged to try reading the sentences with each possible pronunciation and ask themselves which one sounds right.

Compound Words

A compound word is formed by combining two or more words to form one word with a new, unique meaning. Examples of compound words include *houseboat*, *moonlight*, and *basketball*.

Identifying compound words rapidly can assist readers with decoding multisyllabic words. Identifying the smaller, known words contained in the compound words will help students decode the words quickly and maintain fluency.

To teach students to identify compound words, they can practice breaking them into parts. Compound words can be provided using letter tiles, magnetic letters, or in writing, and students can be asked to split them into the two smaller word parts. Puzzle cards can be created with which two smaller words join together to create a compound word. Readers can also be asked to find and mark compound words in texts. When readers struggle to decode compound words while reading independently, teachers can ask what smaller, known words they see in the unknown words.

Teaching Word Analysis Skills and Vocabulary to English Language Learners

Focusing on cognates is one way to help build word analysis skills and vocabulary for English language learners (ELLS). Cognates are words in different languages that share the same roots. For example, the English word *directions* and the Spanish word *direcciones* are cognates. ELLs can be encouraged to look for known parts of unfamiliar words. They can then use knowledge about the meanings in their native languages to determine the meanings of the English words. This strategy

Copyright © Mometrix Media. You have been licensed one copy of this document for personal use only. Any other reproduction or redistribution is strictly prohibited. All rights reserved.

builds upon ELLs' prior knowledge. Explicitly teaching common roots and affixes can help ELLs quickly increase their vocabularies as well.

Scaffolding should also be provided when introducing ELLs to new words. This can be done using visuals that help demonstrate the meanings of the words. Real objects, pictures, and gestures can all be used. Graphic organizers can also be used to show how new words are related and how they connect to specific topics.

Teaching Word Analysis Skills to Struggling Readers

Struggling readers require consistent and explicit instruction, which often includes a combination of both whole-class instruction and targeted individual or small-group instruction daily. They also need frequent opportunities to manipulate words. Both building and breaking apart related words using letter tiles can help struggling readers develop understandings of patterns in the ways words are made.

Struggling readers can also benefit from explicit instruction on chunking words into component parts. Depending on the ages and prior knowledge of the students, this might include identifying syllable patterns, onsets and rimes, roots and affixes, or smaller sight words that are part of the larger words.

Struggling readers also need frequent opportunities to practice their word analysis skills using real texts. After explicit instruction on recognizing prefixes in words, for example, students can read texts that contain several prefixes. They can identify these words and their meanings. This will help them transfer their word analysis skills to realistic contexts. Scaffolding can be provided through anchor charts, graphic organizers, and teacher support during these independent reading experiences to provide reminders of known strategies.

Teaching Word Analysis Skills to Highly Proficient Readers

Proficient readers still have a need for differentiated reading instruction, even if they are meeting or exceeding grade-level expectations. They can benefit from developing the same word analysis skills as other readers, such as looking for known parts in unfamiliar vocabulary words, breaking words into components, and finding relationships between the meanings and spellings of different words. These strategies should be presented using materials and interactions that are both engaging and appropriately challenging for proficient readers. Use of texts that have some unfamiliar words will ensure that readers have opportunities to apply these strategies and continue to increase their vocabularies. Using assessments to determine reading levels or teaching readers to self-select appropriate texts can help ensure that the selected materials offer some challenges and learning opportunities for proficient readers.

Because proficient readers often devote less energy to decoding words than struggling readers, they are able to allocate more energy to reading comprehension, analysis, and reflection. Proficient readers can be asked to evaluate authors' word choices and discuss the effect that certain words have on the meaning or tone of the texts.

Assisting Readers with Comprehension Using Graphophonics, Syntax, and Semantics

Proficient readers understand how to use a variety of reading strategies and are able to flexibly apply them to different situations as needed. The types of text a student reads may differ greatly in terms of vocabulary, quality of context clues, picture support, and connections to the reader's prior knowledge. Therefore, the strategies that work to determine an unknown word in any one sentence or text may not work as well in another.

Decoding words using graphophonic clues is one strategy readers use. They consider the letter-sound relationships in the word. Another strategy is to consider syntax, or how the word sounds in the sentence and fits into the overall sentence structure. A third strategy is to consider semantics, or the meaning of the text, to guess the unknown word. To be correct, a guessed word should fit all three criteria. It should look right (graphophonics), sound right (syntax), and make sense (semantics).

When they come to unknown words, proficient readers try one strategy first and then cross-check their guesses using other strategies. If they realize they have made errors, they self-correct. Using a combination of these strategies helps ensure that readers make sense out of what they are reading.

Helping Beginning Readers Use Context Clues to Figure out Unknown Words

Like older readers, beginning readers also turn to context clues to figure out unknown words. The types of context clues available to beginning readers may differ, however, because the texts they read often contain simple sentence structures and picture support.

One strategy beginning readers can use is to look for picture clues. When a reader is stuck on an unfamiliar word, the teacher can guide the student to look to the picture for hints.

Another strategy is to ask the reader to skip the unknown word and read the rest of the sentence. After finishing the sentence, the teacher can ask the reader to fill in the blank with a word that makes sense. Context clues found in the rest of the sentence can often help the reader guess the missing word. If the reader guesses a word that makes sense but does not match the text, the teacher can guide the student to look for phonetic clues within the word, such as the first sound, and try again.

Texts for beginning readers sometimes contain other context clues, such as rhymes and repetitive vocabulary, that can be used to figure out unknown words.

Types of Context Clues

There are several different types of context clues that are often provided in sentences. One common type is a definition clue. In this type of clue, a definition for the unfamiliar word is provided somewhere within the same sentence; for example, the precocious toddler surprised her parents by learning to read at a much earlier age than her peers.

Another type of context clue is an antonym clue. In this type of clue, an antonym or contrasting definition of the unfamiliar word is provided somewhere within the same sentence; for example, unlike his amiable coworker, Mark was quite unfriendly when interacting with customers.

Synonym clues are a third type of context clue. In this type, a synonym for the unfamiliar word is provided somewhere within the same sentence; for example, the altruistic donor was so selfless that she donated all of her lottery winnings to her favorite charity.

Inference clues are another type of context clue. With this type of clue, the unknown word's meaning is not explicitly given, and the reader must infer it from the context of the sentence; for example, Sam was thirsty after hiking the three-mile trail, so he ordered a cold beverage at the café.

Helping Students Use Context Clues to Figure out the Meanings of Unknown Words

Teachers should explicitly introduce students to different types of context clues, including definition, antonym, synonym, and inference clues. Examples of sentences containing each type can be provided, and students can be asked to mark the clues, label each type, and explain the meanings of the unknown words. They can also be asked to find examples of each of these types of context clues in other texts. An anchor chart listing the different types of context clues and examples of each can also be posted in the classroom.

Students can also be given sets of words that are related in some way, such as pairs of synonyms or antonyms. They can be asked to write sentences that incorporate the word pairs, creating context clues for other readers. They can then share their sentences with peers, asking them to identify the context clues and meanings of the unknown words.

Importance of Knowing Latin and Greek Roots

Many English words are formed from Latin and Greek roots. Therefore, recognizing these roots and knowing their meanings can help readers with both decoding and comprehending.

When readers automatically recognize Latin and Greek roots, they will be able to quickly decode the main parts of words containing them. If they automatically recognize the affixes as well, they will be able to break the words into parts and decode the words effortlessly. This will allow the readers to maintain speed and fluency while reading.

The roots also hold most of the meaning in words and form the bases of entire word families. Knowing the meanings of these roots will help readers quickly determine the meanings of many newly encountered words, especially if they also know the meanings of any attached affixes. For example, if readers know that the Latin root *port* means to carry, they will have clues about the meanings of the words *transport*, *transportation*, *import*, and *export* as well.

Helping Readers Identify Latin and Greek Roots in Unfamiliar Words

When teaching readers about Latin and Greek roots in English words, one strategy is to help them see the relationships between words in the same word families. This can be done by creating charts or other visual representations of word families and their meanings. For example, a root and its meaning can be written in the middle of a web, and words containing the root and their meanings can be written in circles branching off from the root.

Another strategy is to create three sets of cards, including prefixes, suffixes, and roots. Students can experiment with combining the sets of cards to try to form real words. When real words are created, students can explain their meanings. Students can also be given words containing prefixes, roots, and suffixes. They can be asked to break the words into their components and identify the meanings of each part.

Additionally, students can be encouraged to locate words containing Latin and Greek roots in the texts they read independently. They can use their knowledge of the roots to define the words.

Affixes

Affixes are letters or groups of letters that are added to root words. Prefixes and suffixes are two common types of affixes. Root words may have one or multiple affixes attached to them.

Learning to identify affixes and understand their meanings is important for both fluency and comprehension. Because the same affixes are used repeatedly in English, immediately recognizing them and knowing how they are pronounced can assist readers with decoding multisyllabic words. Decoding the words quickly will help the readers maintain fluency. Because affixes also have predictable meanings, understanding these meanings can help readers comprehend new words in texts and build vocabulary. For example, if readers encounter the word *declutter*, they may know that *de* means the opposite of something, and *clutter* means a messy collection of things. Using this knowledge, they can put the parts together and determine the meaning of *declutter*.

Prefixes

A prefix is a letter or group of letters added to the beginning of a root word. The prefix modifies the existing word's meaning, and a new word is formed. For example, the prefix *dis-* can be added to the word *respect* to form the new word *disrespect*.

Students need to understand the difference between a prefix and base word. It should be emphasized that the base is a whole word, whereas the prefix is a letter or group of letters that cannot stand alone. Examples of words containing prefixes can be provided, and students can practice identifying both the prefixes and root words. Non-examples can also be provided, such as the word *decal*. *De-* is not a prefix in this example because *cal* is not a word on its own.

The meanings of different prefixes can then be introduced. Root words can be presented, and their meanings discussed. Prefixes can then be added, and students can discuss how the meanings of the words change. They can list other words containing the same prefixes, along with their meanings.

Students can also be encouraged to find examples of words containing prefixes in texts independently and use clues to determine their meanings.

Suffixes

A suffix is a letter or group of letters added to the end of a root word. When added, it sometimes changes the meaning of the root word and forms a new word. It may also change the part of speech of the root word. An example of a suffix is *-ful*. When added to the end of the root word *thank*, it forms the word *thankful*, which means full of thanks.

To introduce the topic, students can be given lists of words containing suffixes and asked to identify what the words have in common. The suffixes can then be identified, and teachers can explain how the suffixes change the root words. Three-column charts can be created, with columns dedicated to suffixes, their meanings, and example words. Students can be given cards containing root words and suffixes, and they can experiment with pairing them. They can explain whether the combinations form real or nonsense words and define any real words they create. Students can be encouraged to find examples of words containing suffixes and identify their meanings based on context clues in the texts.

Derivational vs. Inflectional Affixes

Derivational affixes are letters or groups of letters added to root words to change the meanings of the words or the parts of speech. For example, if the affix *un-* is added to the root *kind*, the new word *unkind* is formed. Both the original and newly formed words are adjectives, but the meanings of the two words are different. However, if the affix *-ment* is added to the root word *fulfill*, the new word *fulfillment* is formed. The original word is a verb, and the newly formed word is a noun. Both of these examples demonstrate derivational affixes.

Inflectional affixes do not change the part of speech of a word, but they do serve a grammatical function. Inflectional affixes include the suffixes *-s, -ed, -ing, -en, -'s, -er,* and *-est.* For example, adding an inflectional affix can change the word *walk* to *walked.* The part of speech does not change as both words are verbs. The affix only changes the tense of the verb. Inflectional affixes can indicate whether a noun is singular or plural, the verb tense, superlatives, or possessives.

Relationship Between Knowledge of Roots and Affixes

Knowledge of roots and affixes and the use of context clues are closely related. Proficient readers use a combination of these strategies to determine the meanings of unknown words, check their initial guesses, and revise their guesses if necessary.

When encountering an unknown multisyllabic word, a reader may first look for known parts of the word. This may lead the reader to break the word down into the root and affixes. Using knowledge of what each of these components means, the reader may then guess the word's meaning.

However, both roots and affixes can have multiple meanings. The reader's initial guess may not make sense in this particular context. Therefore, it is important for the reader to also consider context clues to check the guessed meaning. If it does not fit the context, the reader may consider other meanings of the root and affixes that better fit the context clues.

The reader may also begin by guessing the word's meaning using context clues and then use knowledge of the root and affixes to check the initial guess. Teachers should encourage readers to use both of these strategies to check and self-correct their guesses.

Reading Comprehension

A basic definition of reading comprehension is understanding what has been read. However, reading comprehension is quite complex. It involves both taking meaning from the text and creating meaning by integrating the text with prior knowledge. It is an active process that requires the use of multiple skills and strategies, such as decoding, fluency, understanding word meanings, predicting, inferring, and more. It involves different levels of understanding, including comprehending both the literal meanings of the words and the unstated themes and implications of the text. Comprehension is one of the main goals of reading instruction.

Comprehension is essential to developing proficient readers. If readers are able to decode the words but cannot comprehend the messages, they won't make any meaning from the texts and will become easily frustrated. Because comprehension is an active process, it is also important for developing engaged readers who enjoy reading for a variety of purposes.

Boosting Reading Comprehension in Ells and Struggling Readers

It is helpful to build background knowledge before introducing new texts to English language learners (ELLs) and struggling readers. Readers can then draw upon this background knowledge to make meaning from the new texts. After assessing what students already know about the topics, background knowledge can be developed using other texts, charts, graphs, photographs, videos, discussions, and additional methods.

ELLs and struggling readers can also benefit from previewing new texts before reading them independently. This may include picture walks or receiving text outlines, which identify the main ideas covered in each section.

Pre-teaching vocabulary can also help ELLs and struggling readers comprehend new texts. Teachers can introduce the vocabulary words and use photos or real objects to help explain their meanings. The vocabulary words can be frequently incorporated into class discussions to familiarize students with them.

Additionally, graphic organizers can be used to help ELLs and struggling readers identify and organize key parts of texts that assist with comprehension. To offer scaffolding, partially completed graphic organizers and/or sentence stems can be provided initially, and support can be gradually withdrawn over time.

Boosting Reading Comprehension in Proficient Readers

Proficient readers can be frequently encouraged to comprehend at the inferential and evaluative levels in addition to the literal level. They can be asked to analyze texts deeply and make inferences, draw conclusions, and form evaluations. They can also be encouraged to complete activities that require higher-level thinking skills. Rather than listing the main characters, for example, proficient readers can be asked to retell the stories from each character's point of view or evaluate the choices the characters made.

To challenge proficient readers and encourage them to be enthusiastic about reading, they can also be given choices about book selection. Teachers can guide students in expanding their text selections to include different topics and genres but allow them to make their own selections. Teachers can also guide and encourage students to choose texts that are appropriately challenging. Proficient readers can also benefit from ownership in reading-related activities. Teachers can create menus of challenging questions or projects that readers can choose from based on their interests.

Engaging in Collaborative Discussions About Print and Digital Texts

Engaging in collaborative discussions can have several benefits for readers. It allows them to learn from other people's experiences and perspectives, which may differ from their own. Readers may hear additional evidence that strengthens their own initial understandings and conclusions. Conversely, they may hear evidence that challenges their initial thoughts and requires them to make revisions. Readers also have to support their points with text evidence to explain their thoughts to classmates. Locating and analyzing text evidence can assist with comprehension.

Discussing texts with others also has broader social benefits. It gives students opportunities to be active and social learners. Sharing ideas and collaborating helps build a community of learners who are able to share and respect different points of view. It also allows students to experience different social roles within the group and develop conflict resolution skills.

Methods of Structuring Collaborative Discussions About Print and Digital Texts

Literature circles are one way to structure collaborative discussions about print. Literature circles consist of small groups of students who lead discussions about shared texts, which may or may not have been self-selected. Students collaboratively analyze the texts, discussing topics such as character development and theme. In some classrooms, guiding questions are provided by the teachers, whereas discussion questions are student generated in others. Sometimes students are assigned roles within the group, such as summarizer and discussion leader.

Other times, there may be <u>whole-class collaborative discussions</u> about print. These types of discussions may occur when the whole class is completing an author study, for example, and are comparing and contrasting the events of different texts. These discussions are typically teacher led.

There may also be small-group, teacher-led, collaborative discussions about teacher-selected texts. For example, discussion time may be included during guided reading groups.

Influence of Culture on Reading Comprehension

Culture affects the ways people view and interact with the world around them. As a result, readers of different cultural backgrounds may comprehend the same texts differently. Readers rely on prior knowledge and existing schemata to make sense of what was read. Texts that are culturally familiar and related to readers' existing cultural schemata are more easily comprehended than those that are unfamiliar. When reading culturally familiar topics, readers are better able to make predictions, inferences, and conclusions based on existing schemata.

Therefore, it is important for teachers to activate both students' content knowledge and cultural knowledge prior to reading. For example, students may read a text describing a birthday celebration. The teacher can activate students' knowledge about how birthdays are celebrated in different cultures.

Research has indicated that cultural differences in syntactic complexity are less likely to affect comprehension.

Reciprocal Teaching Strategy

Reciprocal teaching is a strategy designed to assist students with reading comprehension. In reciprocal teaching, students and teachers share the responsibilities of leading small-group discussions about texts. Teachers initially take the lead and model using four main comprehension strategies, including generating questions, summarizing, clarifying, and predicting. They gradually share more responsibility with students, who eventually take over leading the groups in applying these strategies to analyze texts.

Reciprocal teaching has several benefits. It requires students to be actively engaged in the reading process, as they must understand and apply the reading strategies to guide their classmates. It encourages the use of higher-level reading strategies that can then be applied to other texts. It also encourages discussion and collaboration among class members. Additionally, reciprocal teaching can help build students' confidence in their abilities to independently read and analyze challenging texts.

Inferring

Authors sometimes provide clues in their writing rather than stating things explicitly. When this occurs, readers must make inferences or draw conclusions based on facts, prior knowledge, or text evidence rather than explicit statements. For example, an author might state that a character marched off and slammed the door. Although the author did not state it directly, readers may infer that the character is angry based on his actions.

Making inferences is important for comprehension because much of the meaning in a text can be stated indirectly. If readers comprehend only direct statements, they may miss out on major themes or events in the story.

Because prior knowledge can be used to make inferences, it is helpful for teachers to activate students' prior knowledge before reading through previewing and discussing what is known about the topic. Providing students with frequent opportunities to read varied texts can also build prior knowledge that will assist with inferring.

Teachers can also show pictures to students and ask what inferences they can make based upon picture clues. Additionally, teachers can model thinking aloud while reading, discussing what inferences they are making and what prior knowledge, facts, or text clues they are using as evidence.

Drawing Conclusions

Drawing conclusions is important for reading comprehension because it helps readers understand important events or concepts in a text that are not directly stated. Drawing conclusions about an author's purpose for writing can also help readers better evaluate the text because they will be aware of potential bias.

To help readers learn to draw conclusions, teachers can provide students with several supporting details about common topics and ask what conclusions they can draw. For example, they could describe a house with balloons, streamers, presents, and a cake in the kitchen, leading to a conclusion that it is somebody's birthday. A graphic organizer can be used to organize this information, with the conclusion in the middle and the supporting details branching off from this conclusion. This process can then be repeated using details found in texts. This will show readers how they can use prior knowledge and text evidence to form conclusions when they read independently.

Metacognition

Metacognition is when readers think about their own thinking. Proficient readers continuously self-monitor their own reading. They ensure that they are making meaning from the text. If things do not make sense, they use strategies to self-correct the issues. Metacognitive strategies are important for reading comprehension because they ensure that readers are actively engaged while reading and that they understand what they have read. Modeling these strategies by thinking aloud is an important way to help students learn and apply these strategies in their independent reading.

Metacognitive strategies before reading include previewing the text, making predictions, and setting a purpose for reading. Metacognitive strategies during reading include visualizing, making connections, rereading to clarify confusion, and asking self-monitoring questions. Readers also utilize text features to locate and make sense of key information. Metacognitive strategies after reading include summarizing, drawing conclusions, and determining if any unanswered questions remain that need additional clarification.

Activities Promoting Reading Comprehension

Before reading, teachers can set the purposes for reading and activate students' prior knowledge by making connections to what they already know. They can preview the texts and important vocabulary words and encourage students to make predictions.

During reading, teachers can model thinking aloud to demonstrate how they monitor their own understanding. They can check and revise predictions, make inferences, and form connections. They can provide students with guiding questions or graphic organizers to use as they read independently to encourage the same reading behaviors.

After reading, teachers can model summarizing, drawing conclusions, and evaluating the texts. They can also discuss how their thinking changed as they read and were presented with new evidence. They can encourage students to use the same strategies after reading independently by setting up literature circles, creating written response activities, and designing other reading response projects.

Types of Connections Readers Can Make to Texts

Readers can make text-to-text connections. These are connections made between two or more different texts that have been read. Readers might make connections between the texts' events, characters, themes, or any other features. An example is when a reader identifies that characters in two different books both persisted to overcome challenges.

Text-to-self connections refer to connections readers make between texts and their own personal experiences. An example is when a reader understands the sadness a character feels when losing a pet after having personally experienced the same thing.

Text-to-world connections refer to connections readers make between events in texts and events that have happened in the real world. An example is when a reader makes connections between a text about an astronaut and news about a recent space launch.

To encourage readers to make these connections, teachers can model their own thinking during shared reading experiences. They can model thinking deeply about similarities rather than making surface connections. For example, rather than pointing out that two characters are both girls, they can compare their character traits. Teachers can also encourage the use of Venn diagrams to show the similarities and differences between two texts, people, or events.

Benefits of Comparing Different Books by the Same Author

When students read and compare multiple books by the same author, they use several reading strategies important for comprehension. They compare and contrast story elements between texts, such as characters, settings, problems, and solutions. They make text-to-text connections. They also consider how the author's life experiences may impact his or her writing style and content.

After completing multiple author studies, readers may also begin to identify favorite authors. These authors can serve as mentors for students, providing models of how to use language and incorporate story elements in their own writing. The connections readers feel to their favorite authors can also boost engagement with reading and encourage them to seek out additional texts. Students can also learn about the authors' lives and the paths they have taken as writers. They may be inspired by learning that people similar to themselves have become published authors.

Benefits of Learning About Topics Using Different Texts and/or Genres

Reading different texts on the same topic can give readers a more comprehensive understanding of the topic. Each text reflects the personal writing style and bias of the author. Reading multiple texts allows readers to hear different perspectives and form their own judgments.

Reading texts from multiple genres about the same topic is also beneficial. Each genre presents the information differently and serves unique purposes. Reading an informational text about the Civil War may provide readers with an understanding of the war's causes, events, and major figures. Reading a historical fiction book written from the perspective of a soldier may give readers a more personalized account of this period in time, engaging the readers and helping them form personal connections.

When reading multiple texts, readers also need to identify the important points from each and synthesize the information. They need to consider the authors' purposes for writing. These skills assist with reading comprehension.

Summarization

Summarization refers to providing a concise description of the main idea and key details of a text. Summarization assists with comprehension by helping readers separate important information and vocabulary from unimportant information. It also helps readers remember what they have read.

Summarization is often a difficult skill for students to learn. Their initial summaries may provide too few or too many details from the text. Modeling and explicit instruction can help students learn to provide effective summaries. Students can be taught to reread a text and cross off unimportant or repetitive information. They can then be encouraged to locate and mark the main idea and key details that are essential to understanding the meaning of the text. Additionally, they can be encouraged to substitute general words for lists of related words in a category. For example, rather than listing all of the animals belonging to a character's family, students could use the word *pets* instead.

Readers can also complete graphic organizers to develop their summaries. One common type of graphic organizer asks students to complete the following sentence stems to form summaries: Someone, Wanted, But, So, Then.

Role of Prior Knowledge in Reading Comprehension

Research has shown that students learn best when they can relate new information to existing knowledge already stored in long-term memory. This helps them organize and make sense of the new information and apply it in future situations. When reading, prior knowledge can help students determine the meanings of unfamiliar vocabulary words, form predictions about what might happen next, make inferences, and make sense of story events. All of these skills are important for comprehension.

To activate students' prior knowledge, the teacher can ask what students already know about a topic when it is introduced. Students' contributions can be listed on a chart or graphic organizer. Know, want, and learned (KWL) charts can be completed, listing what students already know, want to know, and learned about the topic. The teacher can also ask students to make comparisons by asking how the new topic is similar to and different from something they have already learned.

Denotative vs. Connotative Meanings

Words often have multiple meanings. Denotative meanings are the literal meanings of words. Connotative meanings are the secondary meanings of words and refer to the positive and negative associations that arise from them. For example, the denotative meaning of the word *heart* is a muscular organ in the circulatory system that pumps blood. A connotative meaning of the word *heart* is love.

There are several reference tools that can be used to locate the meanings of words. Dictionaries can be used to find the denotative and connotative meanings of words, along with other information like word origin and pronunciation. Thesauri can be used to find lists of synonyms for words, and antonyms are sometimes included as well. Glossaries list the definitions of important vocabulary words and are often found at the ends of texts. All of these reference tools can be found in both print and digital forms.

Graphic Organizers That Promote Reading Comprehension and Analysis

Know, want, and learn (KWL) charts can be filled out before and after reading to identify what readers know, want to know, and learned about a topic. These charts help activate prior knowledge and give readers a purpose for reading. Story maps can be used to help readers identify the main elements of a story, such as characters, setting, problem, events, and solutions. Character maps can be used to describe traits of characters in the story.

Other graphic organizers can be used to help readers explain the relationships among events or ideas in a story. Graphic organizers can be used to help readers identify the problem and solution in a story, along with the events that led to the solution. Other graphic organizers can be used to record inferences and the text evidence used to make them. Graphic organizers like webs can be used to record the main idea and supporting details of a story. Venn diagrams can also be used to compare and contrast two stories, characters, or other elements.

Importance of Being Able to Recognize Faulty Reasoning in Nonfiction Texts

Faulty reasoning occurs when conclusions are not supported by facts and evidence. The ability to recognize faulty reasoning is important because it helps readers evaluate the claims made in texts to determine if they are factual or not. It also helps readers identify potential author bias.

To assist readers with recognizing faulty reasoning, teachers can explicitly teach several different types and provide examples of how they are used in real texts. Overgeneralizations occur when authors draw conclusions based upon insufficient data. An example is stating that all fourth graders must like pizza because one fourth grader likes pizza. Personal bias occurs when authors base conclusions on personal opinions rather than factors or data. Illogical conclusions occur when authors draw conclusions about the relationships between things without data supporting the relationships. An example is stating that because someone was outside in the rain and later got a cold, the rain must have caused the cold.

Students can be encouraged to locate and share examples of faulty reasoning found during their independent reading experiences. They can also be encouraged to verify the sources used by authors to validate their claims and be wary of unsubstantiated online sources.

Distinguishing Between Facts and Opinions

Facts are statements that can be proven to be true. For example, stating that George Washington was the first president of the United States is a fact. Opinions are statements that cannot be proven true or false. They represent people's judgements or views of something. Stating that cats are easier to take care of than dogs is an opinion.

It is important for readers to distinguish between facts and opinions. Recognizing when statements are opinions can help readers identify any biases the authors may have and recognize that the authors may be trying to persuade them. Distinguishing between facts and opinions is important when reading any texts, but it necessitates special consideration when using digital sources. Anyone can post information online, and readers must be able to evaluate the sources effectively to determine if they are based on fact or opinion.

To teach students to identify facts and opinions, teachers can introduce the terms and provide examples of each. Students can be asked to mark examples of facts and opinions in texts using different colors. They can also be encouraged to look for key words that signal opinions, such as *think*, *believe*, *feel*, *best*, and *favorite*.

Reading Different Types of Text

Literal Comprehension

Literal comprehension refers to understanding the written meaning of a text. It involves a basic understanding of the text's vocabulary, events, main ideas, and other features. Literal comprehension is important because it is the foundation upon which deeper levels of comprehension are formed.

Promoting Literal Comprehension

Answering literal comprehension questions using text evidence is one strategy to support development of this skill. This can be done through class discussions or written activities. Readers can be asked to identify the setting of the story, main characters, sequence of events, or other topics for which the answers can be found directly in the text. Readers should frequently be asked to provide text evidence for their answers, which might involve marking the sentences where the answers are found. Graphic organizers, such as story maps and problem/solution charts, can also help students develop literal comprehension skills.

To scaffold the development of literal comprehension, the teacher can begin by asking questions about a portion of the text immediately after it was read, using the same wording as the text. Over time, the wording can be varied, and the teacher can wait for longer intervals before asking the questions.

Inferential Comprehension

Inferential comprehension is a deeper level of understanding than literal comprehension. It requires inferring what the author meant. The answers to inferential comprehension questions are not found directly in the text. Readers must instead make inferences, draw conclusions, determine points of view, and make other informed decisions based upon the evidence provided in the text.

Promoting Inferential Comprehension

To develop inferential comprehension skills, readers can be asked to frequently make predictions and interferences and draw conclusions. This can be done using class discussions, written activities, or graphic organizers. When making predictions and inferences and drawing conclusions, readers should be asked to provide text evidence to support their choices. This may involve marking parts of the text or recording relevant sentences. They should then be encouraged to evaluate their predictions, inferences, and conclusions as they continue reading. If new evidence conflicts with their initial predictions, inferences, or conclusions, readers should be encouraged to revise them as needed. Proficient readers self-monitor their comprehension and continually revise their understandings as additional evidence is gathered.

Evaluative Comprehension

Evaluative comprehension is a deeper level of understanding than literal comprehension. It requires readers to make judgments and share opinions about what they have read based upon evidence found in the text and prior knowledge. For example, evaluative comprehension questions might ask readers to consider if they would have handled an event in the text differently or explain whether they agree or disagree with the author's point of view.

<u>Promoting Evaluative Comprehension</u>

Because evaluative comprehension requires deeper thinking than literal comprehension, it is helpful for teachers to frequently model their thinking when responding to these types of questions. They can model how to identify relevant information within the text and draw upon prior experiences to form judgements about topics.

It is also helpful to provide readers with evaluative question stems they can reference when reading independently. These question stems can also be displayed on charts in the classroom.

Helping Learners Retell Fictional Stories

There are specific steps teachers can take to focus readers' attention on key parts of stories to assist with retelling. Teachers can preview the stories with students and point out the key events they should listen for before they begin reading. During reading, they can pause and ask students to summarize the key events they have heard in the stories so far. After reading, teachers can lead students in shared retellings or ask students to retell the stories independently.

Students can fill out graphic organizers or create flip books that describe what happened in the beginning, middle, and end. They can also draw or act out the main story events. Additionally, students can be given sentence strips containing the main story events in a mixed-up order and asked to sequence them. Story ropes can also be used, where students tell story events in order as they move their hands along sets of beads or knots on ropes.

Retelling is important for story comprehension because it requires readers to identify and sequence the main story events. Readers must also consider other story elements, such as characters, setting, and plot, during retellings.

Making Predictions

When making predictions, readers gather evidence from the text and pictures and make inferences. They sequence story events and make connections between the text and prior experiences to predict what might happen next. Continually making and revising predictions also helps keep readers engaged. All of these activities support reading comprehension.

To help learners make predictions before shared reading experiences, teachers can conduct picture walks of texts. While showing the pictures, teachers can provide brief overviews of the stories, asking students to contribute their predictions about what each section might be about. During reading, teachers can pause to ask students to summarize what has happened so far and predict what might happen next. Teachers can model using prior experiences, picture and context clues, and memories of similar texts when making predictions.

Readers should be taught to evaluate their predictions to determine if they were correct. They should also be taught to look for additional information that might cause them to revise their original predictions. Readers can fill out charts listing their predictions, the evidence used to support these predictions, and what actually happened in the texts.

Comparing and Contrasting

Readers can compare and contrast many things when reading, such as characters, settings, story events, multiple texts, and more. This supports comprehension because readers must recall details and find text evidence to compare and contrast. Comparing and contrasting also requires higher-level thinking skills and can help readers organize information and clarify confusion between two things.

Venn diagrams are a common way to help readers compare and contrast information. Text evidence and prior knowledge can be used to identify features that are the same and different between two things, and they can then be listed in the appropriate sections of the diagram.

Students can also be taught to identify key words that signal whether two things in texts are the same or different. Word such as *similarly* and *like* signal that two things are the same, whereas words and phrases such as *although* and *on the other hand* signal that two things are different. A chart that lists these key words and phrases can be hung in the classroom as a reminder for students to use when reading.

Genres of Fiction

Realistic fiction stories are about events that could happen in real life. The characters and settings are realistic. Historical fiction stories also contain realistic characters, settings, and events, but they take place in the past, often during important times in history. Mysteries contain crimes or puzzling events that the characters must solve. Fantasies contain story elements that are unrealistic, such as talking animals or magic. Science-fiction stories focus on imagining life with advanced science or technological capabilities and/or extraterrestrial life.

Folktales are another type of fiction. They are popular stories that are passed down from generation to generation, often by word of mouth. Fairy tales are one type of folktale. They often contain magical events and creatures, take place in enchanted places, have happy endings, and have good characters battling evil characters. There are often multiple versions of fairy tales. Cinderella is one example. Tall tales are folktales that include characters with superhuman traits and exaggerated events. Paul Bunyan is an example of a tall tale.

Importance of Being Able to Recognize Different Genres of Fiction

Understanding the characteristics of different genres and being able to correctly classify texts by type is beneficial to readers for many reasons. It assists readers with making predictions because they are aware of the typical text structures of each genre. For example, knowing that fairy tales typically end with good overcoming evil can help readers predict how stories will end. It also helps readers analyze texts deeply and incorporate characteristics of the genres in their own writing.

There are different approaches that can be used to teach about genres. One approach is to complete genre studies in which genres are explored in detail one at a time. Teachers may begin by providing explicit instruction on the characteristics of each genre and then give students opportunities to analyze examples. Teachers may also begin by sharing multiple texts of the same genre and asking students to identify common characteristics on their own. Another approach is to present multiple genres at once using a compare-and-contrast approach. No matter which approach is used, readers should have opportunities to explore many texts of each type of genre to develop an understanding of their common characteristics and text structures.

Analyzing and Interpreting an Author's Craft and Structure

Author's craft refers to an author's style of writing. It includes all of the choices an author makes when writing a text, such as word choice, text structure, point of view, use of literary elements, message, tone, and more. When focusing on author's craft, readers analyze all of these choices and consider the effects they have on readers.

Analyzing and interpreting author's craft and structure helps readers reach a deeper level of comprehension than surface comprehension. It helps them understand how different elements of the text work together to convey a certain meaning and tone. It helps them understand that authors make several deliberate choices throughout the writing process about how to convey their messages most effectively, which will assist readers with making choices in their own writing. Additionally, it encourages active engagement with the text because readers are continuously analyzing and interpreting while they read. Comparing and contrasting author's craft using different texts and authors can also help readers make connections.

Close Reading

Close reading refers to reading and analyzing a text in a thoughtful manner to develop a deep understanding of its meaning, theme, use of language, and other elements. When close reading, readers first read to determine the general meaning of a text. They then reread the text to analyze the use of language and theme. They also make connections between the text and themselves, other texts, or real-world events, and they form evaluations. A goal of close reading is to develop independent readers who are able to form deep meaning from texts with little or no scaffolding. Therefore, close reading activities do not involve previewing, picture walks, or other prereading activities.

Not all texts are ideal for close reading activities. Teachers should choose texts with deep meaning and multiple elements to discuss and analyze. They should consider the complexity of vocabulary, syntax, and meaning when choosing appropriate texts for close reading. They should also consider the complexity of text features and structures.

Teachers can model how to reread texts and analyze different elements each time. They can guide students in this process by asking questions that require increasingly higher-level thinking skills after each reading of the text.

Elements of Poetry

Discussing and analyzing poetry is a common part of literacy instruction. As part of this instruction, teachers can help students learn to recognize common elements in poetry and use the appropriate terminology to describe them.

There are several elements of poetry. A verse is a single line of poetry. Verses can be grouped together to form stanzas. The rhythm in a poem is developed from patterns of stressed and unstressed syllables. Meter refers to a poem's rhythmic structure. Some poems incorporate rhyme, which occurs when words end with the same sounds. Rhymes are often found at the ends of verses. Poetry can also use other literary elements, such as alliteration, similes, and metaphors.

Students can learn much about elements of poetry by exploring different types of poems. Students can be asked what they like or dislike about each poem, and these observations can be used to introduce the elements that are used. Students can also compare and contrast different types of poems to see how the elements can be used in different ways. While discussing these observations, teachers can also introduce the correct terminology and provide additional examples to explain how the elements are used by different poets.

Helping Students Develop an Appreciation of Poetry

There are many ways teachers can make learning about poetry fun and engaging for students. Early childhood and elementary students can be introduced to poetry during read-alouds and shared reading experiences. They can be encouraged to participate by clapping, making hand motions, and joining in the reading. As students get older, they can participate by highlighting and annotating poems and presenting them aloud to others.

Students can also be encouraged to explore different types of poetry to find types that appeal to them. Free verse, sonnets, limericks, haikus, villanelles, and sestinas are just some examples of different types. Students can also be encouraged to experiment with writing their own examples of different types of poetry.

Additionally, teachers can design poetry challenges for students. For example, students can be given magnetic words or print media that can be cut apart. Students can then explore rearranging the words into verses and stanzas to create different types of poems, seeing how the rhythm, meter, and other elements change. Students can also explore poetic elements in favorite songs.

Importance of Being Able to Synthesize

Synthesis is the ability to gather information from multiple sources and combine it to make meaning. It is important because it requires readers to think critically about which parts of texts hold key information. It also requires readers to summarize and put ideas into their own words rather than repeat the texts verbatim. All of these skills assist with comprehension. When readers need to gather information about topics from multiple sources, synthesis is also important. The sources may differ in format and viewpoint, and readers must be able to find and combine the important points from each.

To teach students to synthesize, teachers can model tracking their thinking throughout the reading of a text and explain how it changes as new information is gathered. They can use phrases such as, "I used to think ____, but now I think ____. My thinking changed because____." Text evidence can be cited to explain the changes.

Readers can also be given graphic organizers to fill out as they read, recording key points in their own words. After compiling the key points, students can explain the main ideas they learned from the texts and how their thinking changed as they read.

Encouraging Students to Locate and Use Evidence from Nonfiction Texts

Students can use T-charts while reading nonfiction texts. On the left side, they can record opinions, predictions, inferences, and similar thoughts made while reading. On the right side of the T-chart, students can record the text evidence used to support these thoughts.

Students can also complete scavenger hunts to find text evidence. Teachers can ask students broad questions that require higher-level thinking skills and instruct them to search nonfiction texts to find the answers. Clues in the texts that are used to answer the questions can be highlighted or recorded on graphic organizers.

Teachers can also model this process for students. They can begin shared reading experiences by identifying what questions they want to answer by reading the texts. They can then model stopping when they reach evidence that answers the questions and making annotations as they go. Possible annotations include strong evidence presented by the author and additional questions that have arisen.

Promoting Close Reading of Nonfiction Texts

Close reading activities are designed to help students deeply analyze texts. In all close reading activities, students begin reading without first completing any pre-reading activities. They reread the text multiple times, analyzing different layers each time.

The first time that students read the text, they can be encouraged to determine the overall main idea and supporting details. The second time they read the text, they can be encouraged to analyze the author's craft and the text structure. This might include determining which text structure the author used, identifying the key vocabulary words and their meanings, locating nonfiction text features, and establishing the author's purpose for writing. The third time that students read, they can be encouraged to evaluate the text, draw conclusions, and make connections to other texts, personal experiences, or real-world events.

Teachers can model this process for students during shared reading experiences. They can also provide students with graphic organizers to help them record information during each reading. Additionally, they can encourage students to highlight or make notes in the text to label key information.

Role Reading Fluency Plays in the Comprehension of Nonfiction Texts

Fluency is important in comprehending any type of text. When readers are able to recognize words quickly and accurately, their working memories are available to focus on comprehension. Additionally, their thinking is not interrupted by stopping frequently to decode words.

Nonfiction texts present some special considerations for readers. Unlike fictional texts, which often follow a problem-and-solution text structure, nonfiction texts can utilize many types of structures. Additionally, they may contain several content-specific vocabulary words. Readers who are unfamiliar with these text structures and words may be less able to locate key information and predict what will come next, impeding comprehension.

Therefore, it is important to expose readers of all ages to a variety of text genres and structures. When practicing fluency passages, a combination of fiction and nonfiction texts should be included. Teachers should also model reading nonfiction texts so students will recognize what fluent reading sounds like.

Promoting Comprehension of Nonfiction Texts with Writing Activities

Writing can assist students with comprehension of nonfiction texts in many ways. Students often read nonfiction texts to learn new information or figure out how to accomplish tasks. They can create lists of questions they would like to have answered by the texts and record their answers as they read. They can also add additional questions that are generated by reading the texts.

Readers can also take notes to record the main ideas and supporting details of nonfiction texts. There are many note-taking formats that can be used, and outlining is one common method. Readers can also write text summaries or record the main concepts on semantic maps.

Additionally, there are many written response activities that can be used to encourage the use of higher-level thinking skills. Readers can write evaluations, compare and contrast essays, alternate endings, recommendations, and other similar responses.

Applying Comprehension Strategies to Digital Texts

Digital literacy includes the ability to make meaning from digital texts. Because the use of digital texts is now commonplace, teachers should give students opportunities to interact with both digital and print-based texts frequently.

Readers need to develop the ability to search efficiently. This includes generating lists of questions they want to have answered before they begin searching. It also includes selecting relevant search key words. Once search results are displayed, readers need to be able to scan the options and identify the links most likely to be relevant to their needs.

Digital texts are often nonlinear and contain multiple hyperlinks, so readers need the ability to break down the texts and locate key information. They can be taught to use note-taking strategies. This may involve using digital tools, like highlighting and annotation tools, or using graphic organizers.

Readers also need to develop the ability to identify author bias in digital sources. They should be encouraged to verify the sources and the validity of authors' claims.

Digital communications also vary in formality. Readers need to develop the ability to identify the main points in formal texts, like research articles, and informal texts, like blog posts.

Promoting Comprehension by Building Students' Academic Language

Academic language is language used in school. It is the type of language used in textbooks, class discussions, tests, and other school-related situations. It includes both vocabulary and syntax and differs from social language, which is less formal and structured.

Understanding the vocabulary of academic language is vital to understanding the authors' messages. If readers do not know the meanings of several key words, they will not understand the meanings of the texts and will be unable to analyze them deeply. Understanding academic syntax is also important because it helps students break down complex sentence structure to locate key information.

Students need frequent exposure to academic language and opportunities to use it across all content areas. For example, rather than asking students how texts are arranged, teachers can ask them to describe the *text structures*. Using these terms builds familiarity over time. Additionally, teachers can provide partial scripts that students can use when making presentations to incorporate academic language. To help students see the differences between social and academic language, teachers can also help students translate texts from one type to the other.

Recognizing Main Ideas and Details

Recognizing the main ideas and supporting details of texts assist with comprehension. They help readers identify what the texts are mostly about and determine what messages the authors are trying to send.

Understanding paragraph structure can help readers locate the main idea and supporting details. Readers can be taught that the main idea is typically located in either the first or last sentence of the paragraph.

Readers can be encouraged to locate the main idea and mark it in a unique way. They can then be encouraged to locate all supporting details and mark them in a different way. Main ideas and details can also be written on webs or other graphic organizers to help readers comprehend what they have read. Scaffolding can be provided when readers are first learning to complete these graphic organizers and then gradually withdrawn.

Prereading activities, such as discussing the title and previewing the pictures, can also help readers form initial thoughts about the main idea of a text. They can revise their initial thoughts as they read.

SQ3R Reading Strategy

Survey
Question
Read
Recall
Review

SQ3R is a strategy used to help students comprehend textbooks. The S stands for survey. In this step, students preview the text and note features like headings, graphs, and charts. They use this information to predict what the text is about. In the Q or question step, students reread the headings and convert them into questions. They then predict the answers to these questions. The first R stands for reading. In this step, students read the text and attempt to answer the questions they listed. They may also make annotations to note important points or additional questions. The second R stands for recall, and this step involves summarizing each section of the text immediately after it is read. The last R stands for review. Students attempt to answer their original questions without using the text. If they are unable to answer any questions from memory, they review the text and their notes for assistance.

The SQ3R strategy has several benefits. By surveying the text, students activate prior knowledge and set purposes for reading. Listing questions helps focus students' attention during reading. Annotating helps students analyze and make meaning from the text. Summarizing and reviewing help students remember key information.

Types of Informational Texts

Literary nonfiction texts contain true information about topics but are presented using structures similar to fictional texts. They often include clear beginnings and endings and contain literary elements such as figurative language and imagery. Biographies, memoirs, and travel writing are examples of literary nonfiction.

Expository texts are written to explain things using facts. They are structured differently than literary nonfiction texts. They often contain headings, tables of contents, glossaries, charts, graphs, and similar features. These text structures help readers navigate expository texts and locate specific information quickly. A science book explaining the water cycle is an example of an expository text.

Persuasive texts are written to influence readers. They contain evidence to support the authors' claims. An advertisement urging readers to vote for a specific candidate is an example of a persuasive text.

Procedural texts provide step-by-step directions for how to complete tasks. A manual describing how to complete office tasks using specific software is an example of a procedural text.

Teaching Readers to Identify Different Types of Informational Texts

Readers can look for specific features to identify types of informational texts. These features can be explicitly taught using example texts, and charts outlining each type of informational text and its features can be displayed in the classrooms.

To identify literary nonfiction texts, readers can look for accurate and factual texts that are written using text structures commonly used in fiction. Although true, these texts read more like stories, with clear beginnings and endings. Literary elements such as figurative language and symbolism may also be included.

To identify expository texts, readers can look for common expository text structures, including tables of contents, headings, sidebars, glossaries, charts, and other similar features. Readers should also be encouraged to check that the texts are factual because some fictional texts may contain these text features as well.

To identify persuasive texts, readers can look for key phrases that signal opinions. These phrases include *I believe*, *you should*, and *in my opinion*. Readers can also look for details provided by the authors to support their viewpoints.

To identify procedural texts, readers can look for clues that indicate sequence. This might include numbered steps or key words like *first*, *next*, and *finally*.

Purposes of Nonfiction Texts

One purpose of nonfiction texts is to persuade. In this type of text, authors try to convince readers to adopt their points of view using supporting statements. An article written by a doctor urging parents to limit their children's soda consumption is an example of a persuasive text.

Another purpose is to compare and contrast two things. An essay comparing and contrasting the forms of government in two different countries is an example of this type.

Other nonfiction texts are written to inform. These texts describe and explain topics using facts. A nonfiction book about characteristics of reptiles is an example of a text written to inform.

Some nonfiction texts are written to instruct. These texts explain how to do something. A text about how to change a tire is an example of this type.

Other nonfiction texts are written to narrate real-world events. These texts convey real information in entertaining and/or engaging ways. A personal narrative describing a funny event that occurred on a family vacation is an example of a text written for this purpose.

Adjusting Reading Strategies When Reading Different Types of Texts

It is important for students to self-monitor their reading and adjust their use of strategies depending upon the situation. This will help them focus their attention on key information. It will also help ensure that they are comprehending the text and meeting their expected purposes for reading.

When students are reading fiction, they typically read from beginning to end rather than skipping around. This helps them understand the plot and correctly sequence story events. When reading nonfiction texts to answer specific questions, readers may utilize text features like the table of contents to jump to specific sections. This helps readers locate the desired information quickly.

When students are reading for entertainment, they may read the text at a faster rate than when they are reading to analyze specific literary elements or answer comprehension questions. Slowing the reading rate or rereading passages may allow for deeper interaction with the text.

Features of Expository Texts

Expository texts often contain some common features. These features help readers locate and organize key information. They also provide additional information about the content of the text.

The table of contents and index help readers know what information is presented in the text and on which pages to find certain topics. Titles and headings are used to separate content into sections of related information. Enlarged and/or bolded print is often used to draw attention to these titles and headings. Important vocabulary words are often highlighted or written in bold print to catch readers' attention. A glossary or set of sidebars is often included to provide definitions for these vocabulary words. Photographs or illustrations are used to convey information visually, and captions are used to explain their content. Charts, graphs, and tables are frequently used to present relevant data. Maps are also included to provide additional information about places discussed in the text.

Helping Readers Locate and Identify Features of Expository Texts

There are many instructional strategies that can be used to help readers locate and identify features of expository texts. Leading students in feature walks is one common strategy. Using this strategy, teachers share informational and expository texts with students, previewing each section of the texts together. They point out each of the text's features, such as the titles, headings, table of contents, captions, and charts, and discuss the purposes of each. When reading the texts out loud, they model how to use the features to locate and make sense of key information.

To help readers locate and use these text features independently, charts listing the features and their functions can be posted in classrooms. Students can also be given blank charts they can use to record text features found while reading independently. Additionally, students can be given comprehension questions that require the use of text features to answer.

Nonfiction Text Structures

Some nonfiction texts use a compare-and-contrast structure. In this type of structure, both similarities and differences between two or more topics are explained. Sometimes the author presents each topic separately and then includes a discussion of similarities and differences. Other times, the author weaves back and forth between the two topics, comparing and contrasting different features along the way.

Cause and effect is another nonfiction text structure. In this structure, the author describes an event and provides reasons why it happened.

Another nonfiction text structure is chronological order. An author who retells the details of an event or period of time in the order that they happened is using this text structure.

In the problem/solution text structure, a problem is introduced by the author. Possible solutions to the problem are then discussed.

A description or list structure can also be used. In this type of structure, a topic is introduced. Descriptive details about the topic are then listed.

Purposes for Reading

One purpose of reading is for entertainment, which is known as aesthetic reading. Sometimes readers select texts because they look interesting to read, and they read them just for fun. Selecting a fairy tale from the library for silent reading time and choosing a bedtime story are examples of times students read for entertainment.

Additionally, sometimes people read for information. This is known as efferent reading. It occurs when readers select nonfiction texts to learn something new. This might include learning new facts about a topic or learning the steps needed to accomplish a task. Selecting a book about whales while studying ocean life is an example of reading for information. Reading a recipe to prepare dinner is also an example of reading for information.

Reading to learn opinions is another purpose for reading. This type of reading occurs when people are trying to make decisions about things and look to others for advice. Reading online reviews before purchasing a product is an example of reading for opinions.

Assisting with Comprehension by Recognizing the Author's Purpose

Recognizing the author's purpose can assist with comprehension in multiple ways. First, it can offer the readers clues about the text structures and features they are likely to encounter. If readers recognize that the author is writing to inform, they will know to look for features of informational texts, such as headings and content-specific vocabulary words. If readers recognize that the author is writing to entertain, they will know to pay attention to character traits, plot development, and other features of entertaining texts.

Additionally, knowing the author's purpose can help the reader evaluate the text more effectively. If readers recognize that the author is trying to persuade them, they will know to think critically about any claims that the author makes rather than accepting them at face value.

Knowing the author's purpose can also assist readers with determining if texts will meet their needs. For example, students may need to gather factual background information for a science experiment they are completing. They may preview a text and recognize that it is written for entertainment. They may then decide that the text is not suited to meet their needs in this circumstance.

Teaching Readers to Recognize an Author's Purpose

The author's purpose may be stated either explicitly or implicitly in a text. Readers can be taught to recognize text structures and features that help identify the author's purpose. Texts that are written to entertain often contain interesting characters and engaging plots. They may contain entertaining phrases and humor, and illustrations may be present.

Texts written to persuade usually contain evidence to support the author's points of view. This may include statistics, facts, and/or personal opinions. Readers can be asked if the authors appear to be for or against something to determine if texts are written to persuade.

Texts written to inform often include facts, which may be stated using text, charts, graphs, or other features. These texts may contain captioned photographs to provide additional information about the topics. Content-specific vocabulary words are often present. Readers can be asked if the authors appear to be trying to teach them about something to determine if texts are written for this purpose.

It is also important for readers to recognize that authors may have multiple purposes for writing. Readers may recognize text structures and features characteristic of two or more purposes within one text.

Fictional Story Elements

Fictional texts contain characters. There are both primary characters, who are central to the conflicts and resolutions of the stories, and secondary characters, who play smaller roles. The settings of the stories are another feature. The settings include both the times in history and the geographical locations where the stories occur. Fictional stories also contain problems or conflicts. The conflicts are usually introduced early in the stories to hook readers and encourage them to continue reading. The plots contain the main events of the stories, when the characters work to resolve the problems. The solutions contain the resolutions to the problems, which typically occur toward the ends of the stories. Fictional texts also typically contain themes, which are the underlying messages the authors are trying to convey to readers.

It is important for readers to understand that not all fictional texts contain every element. However, recognizing the common features will assist readers with making predictions and comprehending the texts.

Teaching Students to Identify Fictional Story Elements

A common way for teachers to introduce students to fictional story elements is modeling their thinking during shared reading experiences. For example, teachers may pause their reading when evidence is provided about the story's settings. The teachers may explain what they have figured out about the settings and show students which textual clues they used to make these determinations.

Graphic organizers, including story maps, are commonly used tools that help students locate and record story elements. These story maps typically ask students to locate the characters, settings, problems, events, and solutions in stories. Foldables or flip books can also be used to record these elements. These elements can be recorded using a combination of pictures and text depending on the ages and needs of the students. Students can also fill out these graphic organizers as prewriting activities when outlining their own stories.

Teachers can also ask guiding questions to focus students' attention on story elements before reading. For example, they can ask students to listen for the problem in the story before they begin reading.

Types of Characters Found in Fictional Stories

There are several common types of characters found in fictional stories. However, not all fictional stories contain all types of characters.

Protagonists are the main characters in fictional stories that readers can relate to and want to succeed. Protagonists can be complex characters with both positive and negative traits. Although readers empathize with protagonists, these characters do not always demonstrate admirable behavior.

Antagonists are characters who stand in the way of protagonists accomplishing their goals. Antagonists are not necessarily bad characters and can also have both positive and negative traits.

Flat characters do not change over time. Their actions and personalities are consistent throughout the stories. They are sometimes known as static characters.

Round characters are complex characters who display a range of personality traits.

- 69 -

Dynamic characters change over time, usually as a result of experiencing the events in the stories. Readers can identify changes in these characters as the stories progress.

Analyzing Character Development

Authors of fictional texts present a variety of information about their characters. They describe the characters' physical characteristics, personality traits, hobbies, dreams and goals, and approaches to solving problems. After reading the stories, readers get to know the characters and develop the ability to predict how the characters might react to different types of situations. They also identify the roles that the characters play in the stories, such as being the protagonists or antagonists. Additionally, they determine whether or not any characters have changed as the stories progressed, and they identify reasons for these changes. All of these steps are part of analyzing character development.

Students can be asked to discuss character traits and complete character maps using text evidence from the stories. They can be asked to predict how characters would likely react in other situations, based upon their actions in the stories. Students can also be asked to describe how characters have changed from the beginnings of the stories to the ends, using text clues for support. They can also compare and contrast characters from different texts or the same characters during different periods of time.

Role That the Setting Plays in a Story

Setting plays an important role in a story. It describes both the geographical location where the story takes place and the time in history when it occurs. A well-described setting also has the power to set the mood for the story. It can help readers visualize the story's events and imagine that they are present. This can assist readers with comprehension and increase engagement with the text.

To recognize setting, readers can be asked to identify both where and when the story takes place. They can be asked to locate key words within the story that signal the answers to these questions. To explore setting more deeply, readers can be asked to identify how the story evokes their five senses. Using a graphic organizer, they can explore what the characters see, hear, taste, smell, and feel in the story. They can discuss how the use of these details helps readers visualize the setting, and they can be encouraged to use similar details in their own writing.

Teachers can also find examples of mentor texts with detailed settings. Students can explore the ways that the authors describe the settings and discuss how these details affect readers.

Types of Figurative Language

Similes are one common type of figurative language used to compare two things using the terms *like* or *as*; for example, the child grew as fast as a weed.

Metaphors are another common type of figurative language used to compare two things. Unlike similes, metaphors do not use the terms *like* or *as*. They simply state that one thing is another; for example, the star was a glistening diamond.

Personification is a type of figurative language that gives human characteristics to nonhuman things, such as animals, objects in nature, or ideas; for example, the creek danced across the prairie.

Hyperbole is a type of figurative language that uses exaggeration for effect. The exaggeration is so excessive that it is not intended to be taken literally; for example, if I don't eat now, I will starve to death.

Symbolism is another type of figurative language. In symbolism, a writer uses a physical object as a representation of something other than its literal meaning. The symbol often represents something abstract, such as a feeling or idea; for example, diverging physical paths in a text can represent two people making different life choices.

Helping Students Recognize and Interpret Figurative Language

Some types of figurative language can be identified by recognizing key words. For example, students can be taught to recognize the words *like* and *as* in examples of similes. Students can be taught to recognize sound words, such as *buzz*, in examples of onomatopoeia. Charts displaying these key words can be displayed in the classroom.

Figurative language can also be explicitly taught, with teachers explaining each type and providing examples. Mentor texts can be used to provide examples of each type of figurative language, and students can be encouraged to locate additional examples on their own. When examples are identified, students can be encouraged to analyze the messages the authors are trying to convey through the use of figurative language.

Authors use figurative language to make their writing more descriptive and interesting. Because phrases containing figurative language cannot be literally translated, readers must have adequate background knowledge and/or use context clues to determine their meanings. The ability to recognize and interpret figurative language ensures that readers understand the authors' intended messages and are able to comprehend beyond the literal, surface meanings of the phrases.

Allusion

When authors use allusions, they refer to well-known people or events familiar to readers without describing them explicitly. For example, a character being warned to avoid opening Pandora's box is an example of an allusion. It refers to a commonly known story in Greek mythology, and readers are expected to know the meaning of the statement without any further explanation. Biblical, mythological, historical, and literary allusions are four common types. Allusions are commonly found in similes and metaphors.

To help readers recognize allusions, students can be asked to find examples of allusions in texts and discuss their types and meanings. Additionally, they can explore and evaluate the effects the allusions have on the meanings and tones of the stories. Students can also be taught strategies for using tools to research the meanings of unknown allusions they encounter while reading independently.

Digital Literacy

Digital literacy refers to the ability to communicate effectively using digital sources. It involves many component skills, such as locating, processing, analyzing, evaluating, and creating information in digital form. Information can be communicated digitally through websites, social media sites, apps, digital textbooks, multimedia presentations, emails, texts, and more.

The continually evolving nature of digital communication presents challenges for teachers. Tools, software, and equipment should be selected carefully based upon the ability to help students achieve learning objectives.

Teachers also need to help students locate and synthesize information from multiple sources and evaluate the sources for reliability. Students must also learn to share information responsibly and adhere to acceptable use policies. Additionally, students need to be taught to consider their audiences and purposes for communicating in digital environments, just as they do when communicating through speaking and writing. For example, different language and sentence structure will likely be used in business websites than in text messages. With global business and distance education now common, students also need to be taught how to use Web 2.0 tools to collaborate with others.

Media Literacy

Media literacy refers to the ability to comprehend, evaluate, and create media. Media includes methods of communication, such as newspapers, magazines, videos, television, radio, and books.

Students need to critically evaluate the authors' messages and points of view to determine what biases may exist. They also need to determine whether the information presented is supported by reliable sources. Advertisements and testimonials may contain unsubstantiated information, for example.

Because there are many different types of media, students also need the ability to flexibly apply different comprehension strategies. For example, they may skim through newspaper articles to locate and highlight key information, whereas they may take notes during videos. Teachers should incorporate forms of media into classroom instruction and teach strategies for comprehending and evaluating each type.

Teachers can also allow students opportunities to present their learning using different forms of media, such as creating podcasts, writing newspaper articles, filming videos, and more. Students should be taught to consider which types of media will best convey their messages and reach their intended audiences. In addition to helping students develop media literacy, these project options will also accommodate students who prefer different learning modalities.

Visual Literacy

Visual literacy refers to the ability to comprehend, evaluate, and create visuals. It includes all types of visuals, such as cartoons, photographs, illustrations, graphs, infographics, and maps.

Visual literacy is important from an early age. Before students can read words, they "read the pictures" to tell stories and make predictions. They are later presented with other visuals, such as graphs to explain data in nonfiction texts and infographics on websites.

As with all forms of media, students need to evaluate author bias and verify the sources used to create visuals. For example, they can be taught to consider where the data used to create graphs comes from. Students also need to extract key information from visuals by looking for clues, such as bolded print or use of color. Additionally, students need to be taught about the legal issues involved in creating visuals, including copyright issues. They also need to consider design and aesthetics issues.

Teachers can assist students with visual literacy by presenting information using a combination of print and visual forms and allowing students choices when completing assignments. For example, students can create posters to convince other classmates to read favorite books.

Data Literacy

Data literacy refers to the ability to comprehend, evaluate, gather, and organize data. With the increasing reliance on data analytics to drive business and education-related decisions, data literacy must be addressed in the classroom.

Students need to learn how to read and interpret different representations of data, such as charts, graphs, and tables. They also need to draw informed conclusions from the data and recognize potential author bias and data misuse.

Additionally, students must decide which types of data will be useful to answer specific questions and convey certain information. They also need to determine the most effective ways to gather data and present it to others.

Teachers should incorporate data gathering and analysis into classroom activities across all subject areas. Students can gather data when completing science experiments and create tables and graphs to represent their findings. Teachers can conduct surveys with students and record their responses using poll-generating tools on the web. Mini-lessons can be focused on interpreting and evaluating data found in nonfiction texts.

Financial Literacy

Financial literacy refers to making informed decisions about financial resources to prepare for a secure future. It includes skills such as saving and spending money, creating budgets, and paying bills. It also includes business-related terms like profit, expense, and revenue.

Although financial literacy is commonly linked to math skills like balancing checkbooks, it relates to traditional literacy as well. People must be able to read banking and billing statements and understand their terms and conditions. They must also critically evaluate financial offers, such as credit card deals, and consider authors' biases and underlying intentions. These skills are needed to make informed financial decisions.

While teaching about financial literacy, teachers should include a variety of realistic materials for students to read, analyze, and evaluate. They should be given opportunities to make and justify realistic financial decisions based on research and analysis.

Information Literacy

Information literacy refers to the ability to locate, analyze, and evaluate information. It also refers to the ability to responsibly share information with others. Information can be obtained from a variety of sources, including websites, interviews, newspapers, books, and more.

Students first need to recognize when more information is needed. Teachers can encourage students to self-monitor their thinking and recognize when they need to learn more about topics before drawing conclusions. When planning a school garden, for example, students may recognize that they need to learn more about which plants grow well in their area. They may then consult gardening guides to select plants that are well suited for their climate and soil type.

Once information is located, it needs to be critically analyzed so students can comprehend it. They also need to consider author bias and reliability of sources. When sharing information, students need to ensure that they are using reliable sources and not misleading their audiences.

Technology Literacy

Technology literacy involves the ability to use technological tools, equipment, and software to communicate effectively. It includes using technology to access, analyze, evaluate, and share information.

Technological tools are now commonly used in education, and teachers must dedicate instructional time to teaching students how to use them effectively and responsibly. Teachers can assist students with learning to use technology to locate information, such as teaching them to enter specific key words in search engines and skim the results for relevant matches. They can also teach students how to carefully select which technological tools they will use to accomplish specific tasks. For example, if students want to create visual representations of information for a class project, they may consider and evaluate the effectiveness of different infographic building tools.

Technology literacy also involves recognizing the possibilities and limitations of technology in accomplishing specific learning objectives. Additionally, it involves troubleshooting common technological problems and using technology in ethical and responsible ways.

Teaching Multiple Literacies

Multiple literacies are part of 21st-century learning and business. To be successful, people must effectively process and share different types of information using multiple media forms. Therefore, teachers must devote instructional time to teaching students the skills they need to succeed in this technology-rich environment.

Teaching multiple literacies requires a mixture of explicit instruction, guided practice, and opportunities for application. For example, teachers need to teach students to find supporting details in digital texts. They may explicitly teach this skill during mini-lessons by modeling how they highlight key phrases. Teachers may then ask students to highlight key phrases in digital texts independently while they observe and provide feedback. Students may then be given multiple opportunities to apply this skill throughout the year to complete projects and assignments.

Teachers should also provide opportunities for students to interact with texts of all types and communicate using different media. They can offer choices in projects and assignments as long as instructional objectives are met. This method allows students to pursue their own interests and leads to increased engagement and ownership over learning.

Characteristics of Auditory Learners

Auditory learners easily gather and process information through listening. For example, they may determine main ideas from lectures, assess subtle details from speakers' tones during conversations, and follow oral directions to complete multistep tasks. Auditory learners often enjoy speaking as well, and they may frequently participate in class discussions and conversations.

Teachers can implement many instructional strategies to support auditory learners. They can incorporate read-alouds, discussions, and lectures into classroom activities. They can provide audio versions of textbooks and storybooks. They can also record lectures so students can listen to them later to prepare for assignments and assessments. Teachers can allow students to interview others to gather information, and they can introduce songs, chants, and rhymes to assist with memorization. When designing projects and assessments, teachers can allow students to complete oral reports or presentations. Additionally, they can allow students to think through problems out loud and offer verbal feedback. Directions can also be given orally.

Characteristics of Visual Learners

Visual learners easily gather and process information by observing. They may learn by seeing written words, photographs, models, or any other visual representations of information. For example, they may locate words signaling the main ideas of written texts, summarize events detailed in illustrations, or complete new tasks after seeing the steps modeled.

Teachers can implement many instructional strategies to support visual learners. They can encourage visual learners to take notes when reading new texts or learning new concepts. Notes can consist of words, pictures, or combinations of both. Teachers can also provide written directions to complete tasks, or they can visually model the steps. Additionally, teachers can use photos, realistic objects, diagrams, and other visual materials when introducing new concepts to learners. They can provide graphic organizers to help learners visualize the connections among concepts. When reading aloud, they can share and discuss the illustrations. When teachers are designing projects and assessments, they can allow students to present their learning through multimedia presentations, models, or other visual means.

Characteristics of Kinesthetic Learners

Kinesthetic learners learn best by doing. They benefit from watching people model how to do things and being given opportunities to do things themselves. They also benefit from opportunities to be active within the classroom.

Teachers can implement many instructional strategies to support kinesthetic learners. They can consider active ways for students to learn and practice new concepts. For example, first grade students can trace sight words in chalk and hop along the letters, helping them memorize the spellings. Students of all ages can complete science experiments that allow them to mix, measure, and complete other scientific tasks. During math lessons on comparing and ordering numbers, students can form human number lines and discuss the processes they used.

Classroom arrangements and routines are also important for kinesthetic learners. Teachers can consider flexible seating arrangements and opportunities to move throughout the classroom to accommodate these students' needs.

Characteristics of Tactile Learners

Tactile learning is sometimes viewed as a synonym of kinesthetic learning, but there are some key differences. Kinesthetic learning refers to active learning by doing, and tactile learning refers to learning through physical touch. Tactile learners benefit from frequent opportunities to feel and manipulate items during instruction.

Teachers can implement many instructional strategies to support tactile learners. For example, early childhood students can trace letter cards made of different textures. Students can also be given opportunities to spell words in rice, sand, or other textured materials. Manipulating letter tiles can also be used during word work activities. When completing science activities, students can feel objects and describe their textures. During math activities, students can use manipulatives to explore concepts and solve problems. When teachers are designing projects and assessments, they can also allow students to present their learning using models constructed from types of artistic materials.

Using Instructional Strategies That Address All Learning Modalities

Teachers should consider all learning modalities and accommodate auditory, visual, kinesthetic, and tactile learners within the classroom. This is important for several reasons, including the possibility that each student may display preferences for multiple modalities. Additionally, students can benefit from having information presented in multiple ways. For example, students may learn how to complete new tasks by watching their teachers model the steps. However, if given opportunities to practice the steps themselves, students may be better able to remember and apply them in the future.

Additionally, teachers need to consider the specifics of each concept they are teaching when determining which modalities to address during instruction. For example, it is difficult to teach letter formation using only oral directions. Students benefit from seeing the process teachers use to form each letter and from having opportunities to practice forming the letters independently. When teaching rhyming, auditory instruction is important. All modalities play a role in learning.

Classrooms are also made up of diverse students who prefer different modalities. To meet the needs of all learners, teachers can offer instructional choices and present information in multiple ways. For example, teachers can offer print and auditory versions of texts. Directions can be provided in written form and spoken verbally. Teachers can also offer project choices that allow students to present their learning in oral, written, or visual form.

Helping Students Produce Quality Writing in the Content Areas

In preparation for the workforce and independent living, students must be able to successfully write for a variety of purposes and audiences. This is essential because effective writing is required in many professions. For example, scientists publish research studies, sales professionals write sales reports, and marketing specialists create advertisements.

Going through the steps of the writing process also helps students organize, synthesize, analyze, and evaluate complex information. They must make judgments about what information is relevant and which text structures should be used to best convey meaning. Putting content into their own words also helps students comprehend difficult information and vocabulary. Therefore, writing in the content areas supports comprehension in these areas as well.

Teachers can provide varied types of texts to support learning in the content areas. This may include fiction books, journal articles, diaries, field guides, research studies, maps, interview transcripts, and more. Students should interact with various quality texts and discuss the roles they play in different professions.

The Literate Environment and the Classroom Reading Professional

Print-Rich Classrooms

In early childhood classrooms, print-rich environments contain several books and texts of different genres and topics, including both audio and digital texts. Walls and shelves contain signs and labels to help with classroom procedures and organization. Posters display information related to content students have been studying. Reading, writing, and listening centers are available for students to explore during center time. Puppet theaters and flannel boards are present to encourage oral language and storytelling. There are also many literacy-related materials, such as letter tiles and sight word cards. Word walls are posted.

In print-rich environments, students are also encouraged to share and display texts they have created. They may add their own stories to their classroom libraries or hang up signs they have made. Materials created during shared and interactive reading and writing experiences may also be displayed.

In classrooms for older students, signs and posters are displayed containing academic vocabulary, content students have been studying, and classroom procedures. Written and digital texts from a range of genres are present. There are also ample resources available for students to use to locate and share information, such as computers, tablets, dictionaries, and thesauri.

Print-Rich Homes

An important component of print-rich homes is easy access to developmentally appropriate texts in a range of genres. Although favorite texts can be kept and reread repeatedly, children should also have access to new and changing texts over time as their interests and skills develop. Both digital and print-based texts are commonly found in print-rich homes. This may include books, magazines, newspapers, online literacy games, and digital stories.

In addition to books, print-rich homes also contain a lot of environmental print that children can read. This may include cereal boxes, board game directions, recipes, mail, and more. Exploring this environmental print helps children understand different purposes for reading and writing.

Children in print-rich homes also have easy access to a variety of writing materials, such as paper, pencils, and crayons. Computers can also be available to type texts. Children should be encouraged to write for a variety of purposes and audiences.

Promoting Literacy Development with Dramatic Play Centers

Dramatic play centers are common in early childhood classrooms. These centers allow children to act out realistic situations through play. Examples include pretend restaurants, homes, veterinary clinics, and grocery stores. While engaging in dramatic play, children read, write, listen, and speak for authentic purposes.

As children role-play and interact with other children in dramatic play centers, they develop oral language skills. They engage in conversations and practice using language to accomplish tasks, such as ordering in restaurants. They also listen to peers and follow directions, such as when they are pretending to be restaurant servers.

Children also engage in reading activities in dramatic play centers. Labels and realistic print materials can be included. For example, pretend restaurants may include labeled cabinets and menus. Children also practice writing through dramatic play. For example, children who are pretending to be servers may write down orders on notepads.

Building Literacy Activities into Daily Routines and Activities

Teachers can plan reading, writing, listening, and speaking activities across all subject areas. This can include a mixture of independent literacy activities and shared and interactive reading and writing experiences. Texts focusing on topics that are being studied in all content areas can be accessible in the classroom. Students can also write in all subject areas. For example, they can write the processes used to solve math problems and create travel brochures in social studies.

Teachers of early childhood and elementary students can also plan morning meetings in which daily written messages are read and discussed. Students can share current events and topics of interest with their classmates during these meetings, while other students listen and ask questions.

Early childhood and elementary teachers can also incorporate oral language and listening into daily routines. For example, they may recite specific chants or songs during transitions.

Using Instructional Technologies to Create Classrooms Supporting Literacy Development

There are many ways that instructional technologies can be used to create classroom environments that support literacy development. Computer programs and apps can be used to practice and assess literacy skills, and there are many options that differentiate instruction based on students' existing skills. Many of these programs and apps also save and track students' progress, helping both students and teachers track progress toward goals.

Projectors, document cameras, and interactive whiteboards can also be used to magnify texts so students can follow along during instruction. Interactive whiteboards also allow students to actively participate in literacy activities with classmates.

Digital texts can be used to support listening development and assist students with reading texts that are too difficult for them to read independently. Interactive storybooks that display and track text for emergent and beginning readers can also be used.

There are also many digital tools and software options that can be used to create forms of media, such as slideshow presentations, infographics, digital storybooks, and newsletters. Web 2.0 tools can also be used to help students collaborate on projects, even if they are working remotely.

Activities That Support Reading, Writing, Listening, and Speaking Development

Reading, writing, listening, and speaking are the four main components of English language development. All of these components are important and interdependent. They all play roles in making and conveying meaning, which are goals of literacy instruction.

These skills are sometimes practiced in isolation, such as when students listen to audio texts without any follow-up activities. However, when solving real-world problems, these skills are often used together. For example, doctors must listen to their patients' symptoms, make notes on the patients' charts, and then explain their treatment plans. Therefore, it is important for teachers to plan activities that integrate these four skills.

Project-based learning activities and performance assessments are useful for integrating these four skills. As an example, students could read about the benefits of recycling. They could then speak to the school principal to recommend implementing a school-wide recycling plan, listening and responding to the principal's concerns. They could then create posters to advertise the new program to other students.

Creating School Environments That Promote a Love of Reading

Helping students develop a lifelong love of reading is an important goal of literacy instruction. Teachers can model their own love of reading by talking about their favorite books and authors and modeling their own use of reading strategies. They can share stories of how reading has positively affected their own lives and opened up new opportunities.

Teachers can also help develop communities of readers within their classrooms, making reading a social experience. Fun and interactive read-alouds and shared reading experiences can help create communities of readers, along with organizing literature circles and reader's theater activities. Favorite books can be reread multiple times, with students participating in the reading.

Teachers can also give students frequent opportunities to read books of choice. They can create classroom libraries containing multiple types of texts that students can access easily. Comfortable reading spaces, such as reading chairs and pillows, are also beneficial. Students should also have opportunities to visit their school libraries regularly.

Additionally, teachers can guide students in completing author studies. Students may form connections to favorite authors and seek additional books they have written.

Promoting Successful Independent Reading Experiences at School

Independent reading is beneficial for students' reading development and is sometimes necessary when teachers are working with other students. Therefore, some strategies can be used to make independent reading experiences successful.

It is important to teach students to select appropriate texts that will not lead to boredom or frustration. Some teachers instruct students to apply the five-finger rule. In this approach, students randomly select single pages of text to read. If they struggle to decode five or more words, the books are too difficult. Other teachers inform students of their reading levels and keep labeled boxes of leveled texts available. Students can also be encouraged to maintain personal book boxes that contain several appropriate books that are ready for independent reading time.

To remind students of decoding and comprehension strategies they can use during independent reading time, teachers can display posters in their classrooms. Students can also be given small, personalized copies of these strategies to use.

Additionally, students can be encouraged to analyze and discuss what they have read to build interest and engagement. They can maintain reader-response logs or join literature circles with others who have read the same texts.

Motivating Students to Read

One technique to motivate students to read is to make reading an enjoyable part of the daily routine. This includes designating daily time for reading, providing a comfortable, relaxed atmosphere, helping students select texts of interest, and showing genuine interest in discussing the texts together. This technique is easy to implement, and students who look forward to this reading time as children may continue reading for enjoyment in adulthood. A disadvantage is that some students may not respond to this approach.

Another technique is to use rewards and incentives for reading. Some programs reward students after they have read a certain number of books or minutes. Sometimes students are tested on the books they have read to assess comprehension. Read-athons are one example of this approach. Peer participation, competition, and opportunities to earn rewards may increase short-term motivation to read. Disadvantages include the costs of the incentives and the possibility that motivation will decrease once the rewards are removed.

Teachers frequently use a combination of these techniques by providing daily reading time while also incorporating some incentives for reading.

Family Members' Promoting Reading

Family members can help children make reading a part of everyday activities both at home and while out in the community. Helping children explore environmental print and its purposes is one important step family members can take. They can point out business and road signs while driving, for example. At home, they can help children explore environmental print like food labels, posters, and mail.

Family members can also help children understand how reading is used to accomplish daily tasks. They can ask children to help create and read lists at the grocery store and select meal choices from restaurant menus. While driving, they can ask children to help read road signs to determine which routes they will take. At home, they can read directions together to assemble new toys and follow recipes to prepare shared meals.

There are many benefits to reading with children for authentic purposes. It helps children understand that reading is part of daily life and learn that it can be used for many practical purposes. This approach also blends learning with daily life and real-world tasks, helping engage children in the learning process.

Family Members' Encouraging Oral Language Development

Parents and family members should talk to children frequently from the moment they are born. Children learn how to use language by listening to those around them. Family members can respond to their children's initial sounds and beginning attempts at speech by making eye contact and replying. When children begin speaking words and sentences, family members can respond by repeating what they have said and adding additional information. They can encourage children to imitate their words and actions, using games like peekaboo. Family members can talk about what they are doing and ask their children open-ended questions. They can use varied vocabulary and sentence structure in their speech.

Family members can also engage in word play with children. They can read rhyming and repetitive texts, songs, and poems together, encouraging their children to participate. Additionally, they can retell favorite stories orally and make up stories of their own.

Family Members' Promoting a Love of Reading at Home

Family members can incorporate reading time into their children's daily routines. This can include a variety of types of reading experiences. Sometimes family members can read aloud to their children, sometimes children can read aloud to their family members, and sometimes they can take turns reading. Each of these experiences has its own benefits. Children benefit from hearing their family members reading fluently and using reading strategies, and they also benefit from practicing their own reading skills in safe environments.

While reading together at home, families can read a mixture of new and favorite texts. The experiences should be fun and relaxing, with opportunities to talk about the stories and characters. They can also listen to audio texts together at various times, such as when they are in the car.

Children can also benefit from seeing family members reading frequently and for a variety of purposes. Family members can talk about their favorite books and authors. They can also take children to the library frequently to exchange books.

Promoting Community Involvement in Literacy Activities

Teachers can share information with parents about free story time events in their communities. These events are commonly held at public libraries and bookstores. Teachers can also forge partnerships with their local public libraries. They can inquire about programs that issue library cards to students. Local librarians can also be invited to visit classrooms to read aloud to students and share information about upcoming events.

Teachers can set up community volunteer programs. Community members can be invited to visit classrooms to read with students. Students can also potentially visit senior centers or other locations to read to adults. Local authors and business people who use reading and writing in their jobs can also be invited to visit classrooms to discuss the role that literacy plays in their lives.

Additionally, teachers can encourage students to communicate with community members for authentic purposes. For example, students can send thank-you letters to businesses that hosted field trips or sponsored school events. With parents' permission, student work can also be displayed during community events.

Using Instructional Technologies to Promote Literacy Development at Home

There are many free and inexpensive online games and apps that students of all ages can use to practice literacy skills. These include letter recognition activities, phonics skills practice, digital texts with comprehension questions, and more. School districts that subscribe to certain online programs may provide parents with links and passwords so students can practice at home.

Students can also listen to digital storybooks. Online versions are available that track the text for students and show pictures. Audio versions can be downloaded or checked out from public libraries. Family members can listen to and discuss these stories with their children to practice comprehension strategies.

With guidance and supervision, students can also communicate with others using digital tools. They can create presentations and written texts using word processing and presentation tools. They can communicate with family members using emails, texts, and videoconferencing tools. They can also use free online tools to create and publish their own digital stories.

Increasing Family Involvement in Reading Development

Teachers should communicate with caregivers frequently to increase family involvement in reading development. They should convey to caregivers that they view them as partners and assure them that they welcome questions and concerns. Teachers should frequently communicate positive information to caregivers in addition to sharing reading concerns. Teachers should also recognize that different families have different resources available, so they should try communicating through multiple channels. This may include phone calls, texts, classroom websites, paper newsletters, emails, and more. Teachers should also be aware of scheduling, cultural, and linguistic differences. Information can be sent home in multiple languages, if possible.

Teachers can share links to reading activities and strategies using classroom websites and newsletters. They can also send home reproduceable books and texts from classroom libraries, which students can read with their families. Consumable supplies can also be sent home, such as cardstock letter tiles that can be used to practice spelling and building words.

Parent and family nights can also be scheduled to share strategies and display student work. These events can be recorded and shared with parents who are unable to attend.

Identifying Students Who Have Not Met Standards

It is important to identify concerns with literacy development early to prevent future academic difficulties. Reading, writing, listening, and speaking affect performance across all content areas. Therefore, students who struggle with literacy may struggle in all academic areas.

Early screening is one way to identify students who are not meeting standards and may have literacy difficulties. Depending on the ages of the students, screening can be given on a range of topics, including alphabetic principle, phonological and phonemic awareness, decoding strategies, fluency, and comprehension.

The results of criterion and norm-referenced formal assessments can also be used to identify students who have not met standards. Teachers can look for specific skills and standard areas that students struggled with on these formal assessments. They can also look for indications that students are not meeting their adequate yearly progress goals.

Additionally, informal assessments can be used to identify students who are not meeting standards. Classroom observations, running records, responses during literature circles, and other informal assessments are helpful tools for teachers to use.

All of these data points can be considered when determining which students may benefit from targeted interventions.

Determining Whether Students Should Be Evaluated for Reading or Language Delays

Generally, teachers should collect multiple data points over time before requesting that students be evaluated for potential delays or disabilities. Students may perform below expectations on assessments for a variety of reasons, including illness and fatigue. Therefore, no one assessment score should be used as the basis for an evaluation. However, if students perform similarly on multiple assessments over time, further investigation may be warranted. Assessment data can also be combined with classroom observations for additional information. Additionally, interventions can be attempted first to determine if achievement gaps can be closed through targeted instruction.

Parents also sometimes request that their children be evaluated. Parents are often the first to notice potential issues because they observe their children's progress from year to year and witness the challenges firsthand. Parents can submit their requests for evaluations in writing to classroom teachers, reading specialists, administrators, or other school officials for consideration.

Components of Effective Literacy Interventions

Literacy interventions should be targeted to students' individual needs and based upon assessment data. Interventions can be delivered either individually or in small groups, if multiple students can benefit from the same interventions.

If commercial intervention programs are used, they should be carefully evaluated to ensure they are research based. Interventions should be based upon clear objectives. They should also incorporate ways to measure students' progress to evaluate if the interventions are successful. Pretests are commonly given when interventions are implemented, and the results are used to set goals. Student progress is then monitored regularly to determine if progress is being made toward the performance goals.

Research has shown that frequent interventions are more effective than infrequent interventions, even if they occur for shorter blocks of time. For example, teachers may conduct small-group interventions daily, for 15 minutes each time. Students need frequent opportunities to practice and apply new skills. Interventions should include a mixture of systematic and explicit instruction and guided practice with feedback.

Although students benefit from interventions with classroom teachers and literacy specialists, some carefully selected computer-based interventions may also be used at times.

Evaluating the Effectiveness of Literacy Interventions

Literacy interventions are planned for students based upon assessment data. This initial data is used to set performance goals, and progress toward goals is measured using progress monitoring and intervention posttests. If students make regular progress and achieve their performance goals within the expected time frames, the interventions are usually considered effective. If students make minimal or no progress toward their goals despite receiving interventions, the interventions may be considered ineffective, unless additional factors are impeding success.

However, interventions must be implemented with fidelity to determine their effectiveness. Teachers must use the agreed-upon strategies and instructional methods and meet with students consistently according to their intervention schedules. They must also ensure that the interventions are not interrupted. If issues occur in these areas, lack of student progress may not be the result of ineffective intervention planning. The interventions may have the potential to be successful, but the implementation and delivery methods may need improvement.

Reading Strategies vs. Reading Interventions

Reading strategies and reading interventions are often used interchangeably, but there are some key differences between the two. Reading strategies are methods teachers use to help students learn reading skills. To teach students to comprehend texts, teachers may encourage students to make predictions and inferences. Strategies are taught during regular classroom instruction and may be reinforced individually or in small groups. Meeting informally with a student to review and practice how to make predictions during one class session is not a formal intervention as no set improvement plan, regular meeting schedule, or progress monitoring assessment is involved.

Interventions are specific plans to help students make progress in targeted areas. They are based on assessment data, and they are scheduled for regular, set periods of time. Students' progress is monitored through frequent assessments to look for improvement. Reading strategies may be taught and practiced as part of formal intervention plans.

Signs of Dyslexia

Dyslexia is a common disorder that affects reading. Students with dyslexia often have difficulties with phonological awareness, accurate word recognition, decoding, and reading fluency. As a result, they may also have difficulties comprehending what they have read. Spelling may also be affected. Teachers may notice that students struggle to decode words and read fluently, and students may become anxious or frustrated when asked to read. Dyslexia does not affect intelligence and is marked by a gap between students' abilities and achievements.

Although there is no cure for dyslexia, targeted interventions are often successful. A multisensory approach to reading instruction is often helpful, along with systematic and explicit instruction in reading skills and sight word recognition. The Orton-Gillingham method is one commonly used approach. Teachers should also maintain supportive classroom environments and not rush students or force them to read aloud. Students with dyslexia may also benefit from some accommodations, such as extra time on tests, increased wait time when responding to questions, and access to audio versions of texts.

Signs of Dysgraphia

Dysgraphia is a disorder that affects written expression. Students with dysgraphia may have difficulties holding pencils correctly, forming letters, writing on lines, putting thoughts into written words, and organizing writing in meaningful ways. Handwriting and spelling are also commonly difficult for students. Students with dysgraphia may become frustrated or anxious if asked to write, and they may try to avoid writing when possible.

There are many ways teachers can assist students with dysgraphia. To assist with spelling, explicit instruction on sound-symbol relationships and spelling patterns may be helpful. Graphic organizers can be provided to assist students with written organization. Additionally, students may qualify for occupational therapy to assist with developing coordination and motor skills. Students with dysgraphia may also benefit from some accommodations, such as being allowed to type responses or answer questions orally. They may also benefit from receiving extra time to complete assignments and tests.

Signs of Dyspraxia

Dyspraxia is a disorder that makes it difficult for the body to coordinate movement. Students with dyspraxia may have difficulties with balance and coordination, and they may have trouble performing tasks that require motor skills. Students with dyspraxia may also be sensitive to noise and touch. They may also have spatial and perceptual difficulties, which may affect reading and writing. Some types of dyspraxia may also affect language, especially enunciation.

In the classroom, teachers can break large, multistep tasks into smaller chunks. If activities require movement, teachers can begin with simple movements first, and gradually increase the difficulty. Teachers can also provide extra processing time when giving directions and extra wait time when asking questions. Some students with dyspraxia may qualify for occupational therapy services. Students with dyspraxia may also benefit from certain accommodations, such as seating that is free from noise and distractions.

Characteristics of Reading Comprehension Deficiencies

Students with reading comprehension deficiencies have difficulties understanding and responding to what they have read. They may have difficulties summarizing texts, making inferences, differentiating between main ideas and supporting details, and more. They often have difficulties with reading fluency as well, especially with phrasing and prosody. Students with comprehension deficiencies can often decode words efficiently, yet they struggle with comprehending the texts' meanings. However, some students may struggle with both decoding and comprehension.

To assist students with comprehension deficiencies, teachers can provide advance organizers that offer overviews of the text structures and story events. They can also preview texts or conduct picture walks to familiarize students with the topics. Before reading, they can instruct students to pay attention to specific key information within the texts. Additionally, teachers can model their use of comprehension strategies during think-alouds and shared reading experiences.

Characteristics of Reading Retention Deficiencies

Students with reading retention deficiencies have difficulties remembering what they have read. This may include difficulties summarizing texts, ordering story events, and making text connections after reading. Retention deficiencies may occur due to difficulties transferring information to short- or long-term memory or with difficulties retrieving information that has been previously stored in long-term memory.

To assist students with retention difficulties, teachers can provide students with graphic organizers that they can complete while reading. Story maps and sequencing charts are examples of graphic organizers that may be helpful. Teachers can also provide notes and text summaries to assist students with remembering important concepts and details. Additionally, students can be taught to use specific strategies to activate memory, such as visualizing as they read. They can also be taught to annotate texts by highlighting key phrases and taking notes, making it easier to locate important information in the future.

Role of Social Context in Language Development and Usage

Members of a group have a shared social identity that is formed by reading, writing, listening, and speaking with one another. Group members develop common expressions, mannerisms, and favorite stories that are understood by other members. For example, members of an extended family may use certain expressions when they are together that have been handed down over time. Members of a professional group may use academic language specific to their field at conferences and work events. However, they will not likely use these terms while talking with people outside the field.

Additionally, social context plays a role in how people select the appropriate language to use. When asking a stranger for directions, a person would likely consider social norms and begin with an expression like "Excuse me." When talking with a good friend on the phone, a person might use an informal, joking tone. It is important for people to consider each situation and determine which approach to use.

Teachers can provide frequent opportunities for students to communicate with others for a variety of authentic purposes. This can include communicating with classmates, other students and adults within the school, family members, and community members.

Role of Cultural Context in Language Development and Use

Language involves not only the words people say but also the ways in which these words are interpreted by recipients. Differing backgrounds and cultures can affect how messages are received, and it is important for people to consider that others may view communications differently. For example, in some cultures, students are encouraged to ask questions and initiate discussions in class. In others, students are expected to defer to their instructors and not speak unless they are directly questioned. A student who tells an instructor that something doesn't make sense may be praised for using metacognitive strategies in one class while perceived as being rude in another.

Cultural context also affects how nonverbal communications are interpreted. For example, different cultures have their own norms about making eye contact while speaking and using gestures during greetings.

Teachers should be sensitive to these cultural differences and consider the roles they may play in student participation and communication. Additionally, teachers should help students view situations from multiple perspectives and consider how their attempts at communication may be perceived by others in various situations.

Interdependent Relationship Between Culture and Language

Culture and language influence one another. Language is passed down among members of different cultures, with shared meanings and norms of communication. The ways that people use language and interpret language directed toward them is related to their cultures. Additionally, as cultures change over time, so do languages. Existing words can take on new meanings, and new words may be added to languages. These changes sometimes occur as a result of popular culture, including television, video games, and music. As people with different cultural backgrounds interact, they must negotiate these differences to make meaning.

Because culture and language are so intertwined, understanding the cultural contexts in which language is used is an important part of learning any new language. English language learners (ELLs) should be taught English skills in context, helping them understand how the language is used in realistic social interactions. Additionally, it is important for teachers to understand the cultural backgrounds of ELLs and the roles their cultures may play in their language interactions and expectations. Teachers should also incorporate a variety of teaching strategies and methods into their classrooms to meet the needs of all students.

Characteristics of Advanced Readers

Advanced readers can display many different characteristics. They are sometimes identified by above-average scores on standardized reading assessments. Other times, observed reading behaviors and performances on classroom assignments can provide clues.

Advanced readers typically read fluently and have strong word recognition and decoding abilities. They are also able to flexibly apply a variety of reading strategies to figure out unknown words and meanings.

Advanced readers may also have well-developed vocabularies and incorporate varied words into their speech and writing. They may show a strong interest in reading and get deeply immersed in the texts they have selected. Advanced readers often love to talk with others about the books they have read, and they may make connections between the texts and themselves, other texts, and real-world events. Additionally, they are often able to analyze texts using high-level comprehension skills, such as evaluating and drawing conclusions.

Challenging/Engaging High-Achieving Readers

<u>Collaborative Learning Opportunities</u>

High-achieving readers can often benefit from participating in collaborative, project-based learning opportunities that allow them to apply higher-level reading and writing skills with others. Collaborative projects draw upon the strengths and unique problem-solving abilities of all group members and allow high-achieving readers to work with others to solve realistic problems. They allow students to share ideas and receive feedback from others of all skill levels, including other high-achieving students who may enjoy analyzing and discussing the same types of complex texts that they do.

High-achieving readers can also benefit from forming collaborative relationships with teachers. They can be taught to use metacognitive strategies to self-monitor their own reading and set realistic but challenging goals for their own reading and writing development. They can collaborate with teachers to select literacy projects that pertain to their interests. This involvement in the learning process can help high-achieving readers stay interested and engaged in literacy instruction.

<u>Open-Ended Assignments and Projects</u>

High-achieving readers often benefit from having some choices about what and how they learn. This can include choices about the types and topics of texts they explore. For example, if classes are learning about persuasive writing, students may choose the texts they will analyze from a range of genres and topics.

Students can also have some choices about the complexity of the projects they complete, with options to delve deeper into topics if desired. For example, if students in a class are identifying characteristics of fairy tales, some students may choose to compare and contrast multiple versions of the same tale and note identifying features.

High-achieving readers may also benefit from having choices about the formats of their projects. Possible project ideas include creating multimedia presentations, writing alternative endings to texts, creating three-dimensional artistic representations of story events, and more. These options also accommodate different learning modalities. Teachers may create menu options for students to choose from or encourage them to come up with their own ideas.

Although students may be directing some of their own learning, teachers should still conference with high-achieving readers frequently to assess progress and collaborate on ideas.

Issues and Frustrations of High-Achieving Readers

High-achieving readers are sometimes required to read the same texts as the other students in their classes during reading instruction and in other content areas. Because these texts are often designed for on-level readers, they may be easy for high-achieving readers to decode and comprehend. Without any challenges in the texts, high-achieving readers may finish quickly and possibly become bored.

High-achieving readers are also sometimes given extra work to complete when they finish their on-level work early. They may view this extra work as a punishment, and the new work may not be challenging for these students either. Boredom and frustration may then occur.

Additionally, high-achieving readers may become bored during whole-class lessons on concepts they have already mastered. For example, readers who are successfully decoding complex multisyllabic words will likely become bored during lessons on CVCe spelling patterns.

These high-achieving readers may sometimes appear disengaged, resist coming to school, or have behavior issues within the classroom. To prevent these issues from occurring, teachers can differentiate instruction and provide high-achieving readers with opportunities to read texts within their instructional levels. These students can also be encouraged to complete alternate assignments that are more challenging.

Reading Specialists Support of Classroom Teachers

Reading specialists often play a variety of roles within their schools. Some reading specialists serve as intervention teachers. These specialists directly provide targeted intervention services to students who are struggling with reading, often in areas including phonemic awareness, decoding, sight word recognition, and comprehension. They may go into students' classrooms to provide intervention services, or they may pull students out for a set number of minutes each week.

Reading specialists may also provide professional development opportunities for classroom teachers. In small or large-group sessions, they may model how to use instructional strategies that are supported by research. They may compile literature and resources related to literacy instruction and make these resources available to teachers. They may also work with individual teachers to develop instructional plans or overcome difficulties with literacy instruction.

Reading specialists may also oversee standardized literacy assessments for their schools and train teachers in testing procedures. They may work with teachers to analyze assessment data and use the results to plan appropriate interventions. They may also work with teachers to track students' progress over time and make changes to intervention plans when necessary.

Professional Development Opportunities

Reading specialists may provide professional development opportunities for teachers on a wide range of topics. For early childhood teachers, reading specialists may offer training about modeling concepts of print, planning phonological and phonemic awareness activities, creating print-rich environments, and designing effective literacy centers. Other topics may include types of reading and writing experiences and using multisensory approaches to reading and writing instruction.

Professional development for elementary teachers may include topics such as incorporating reading and writing across content areas, using interactive word walls, using assessment data to guide instruction, modeling comprehension strategies, and designing effective literature circles.

For middle and high school teachers, professional development topics may include teaching academic vocabulary, incorporating reading and writing across content areas, teaching text structures, and using higher-level comprehension strategies.

Reading specialists may also provide professional development opportunities on specialized topics, such as meeting the needs of students with disabilities and teaching reading strategies to English language learners (ELLs).

Leveled Book Rooms

Leveled book rooms are consolidated collections of leveled readers that can be checked out by all teachers within a school. Reading specialists often help organize and maintain leveled book rooms as part of their responsibilities. Because teachers frequently have students who read both well above and well below grade level, these types of book rooms ensure that all students have access to books within their instructional reading levels.

To implement successful leveled book rooms, books should be clearly organized and labeled according to level. The same leveling system used by classroom teachers should be used in the leveled book rooms for consistency. Books may also be organized in additional ways, such as by genre, topic, or author. Teachers should be taught the procedures for checking out and returning books. Records should be kept to keep track of where all books are located.

Promoting the Goals of Schools' Reading Programs to Parents and Family Members

Although it is common for classroom teachers to communicate with family members about reading development, reading specialists also play important roles in promoting literacy at home. Reading specialists may conduct family surveys to learn more about home literacy behaviors and to assess parents' literacy-related needs and concerns. They may help organize school or district-wide family literacy events. These events may offer hands-on literacy activities appropriate for different grade levels that family members can complete with their children and take home for additional practice. They may also feature interactive read-alouds that model ways parents can encourage reading behaviors with their children at home.

Additionally, reading specialists may be involved in organizing book fairs or lending libraries that supplement their schools' traditional libraries. They may provide families with information about summer reading programs. They may also attend parent conferences to provide information about reading goals and interventions.

Promoting Collaboration Among Teachers and Other Colleagues

One role of a reading specialist is to promote collaboration among colleagues. A collaborative approach allows colleagues to develop and work toward shared goals. It can increase motivation to implement reading programs with fidelity and help colleagues share strategies to address common problems and concerns.

In addition to attending staff meetings, reading specialists can attend grade-level team meetings. Reading specialists can help grade-level teams analyze assessment data to identify areas in need of improvement. Together, the teams can create performance goals that will be used to drive reading instruction. They can collaboratively develop instructional plans and activities to help reach the shared goals. This type of collaborative approach can encourage motivation and accountability.

Reading specialists can also look for each colleague's strengths and note strong examples of research-based reading instruction. They can encourage these colleagues to share their strategies and allow others to observe their teaching. Teachers can also be encouraged to share problems they are having with reading instruction, and colleagues can work together to develop solutions to these problems.

Role in Improving Schools' Reading Curricula

Reading specialists typically have access to assessment data from multiple grade levels and time periods. They can lead data analysis teams that look for trends that may indicate gaps in their schools' reading curricula. Once these gaps are identified, reading specialists can work with teachers to revise curricula and instructional methods to better address these needs and improve student performance. Reading specialists often also serve on committees to evaluate and select potential reading programs to supplement or replace existing ones. Reading specialists can share their knowledge of research-based approaches to literacy instruction and use this knowledge to evaluate the potential reading programs.

Reading specialists can also identify external professional development opportunities that may be beneficial for teachers based on their schools' instructional gaps. They can advocate for opportunities for teachers to attend these sessions and share what they have learned with colleagues.

Additionally, reading specialists can recruit teachers who are willing to apply and model specific research-based instructional strategies while receiving coaching and support. For example, reading specialists can recruit teachers willing to try interactive word walls or literature circles.

Building Consensus Among Colleagues When Making Instructional Decisions

Reading specialists often deal with conflict in their roles. Conflict may occur when introducing new reading programs or helping teachers decide upon new instructional strategies and goals. One role of a reading specialist is to help build consensus among the different stakeholders involved, including teachers, administrators, board members, and other school staff.

To help build consensus, reading specialists need to be seen as leaders who are respected in their expertise but also flexible and willing to listen to new ideas. By listening to suggestions and concerns while also explaining literacy-related research and best practices, reading specialists can help their teams develop shared visions for school reading instruction. They can help other stakeholders understand their roles in helping achieve these visions by outlining specific but attainable goals and outlining the responsibilities of everyone involved. Other stakeholders will be more likely to cooperate with the plans if they understand the roles they will play in accomplishing the shared goals.

Resolving Conflict Among Colleagues Regarding Reading Instruction

Instructional decisions have lasting effects on teachers and students. This is especially true when major decisions are made, such as selecting new reading programs. Conflict about instructional strategies and ways to implement change often lead to conflict. Therefore, reading specialists who are facilitating these changes must often assist with conflict resolution.

Reading specialists can first acknowledge the conflicts rather than ignore them, recognizing that conflict can be healthy when it leads to open discussions and sharing of ideas. They can then look for root causes of the conflicts. Although the conflicts may be based on personality differences, they may also be based on other issues, such as concerns about adequate time or resources and differing prior experiences. Helping highlight the true issues may lead to discussions about how the concerns can be alleviated.

Reading specialists can also bring the discussions back to shared performance goals. Colleagues can be asked to restate the shared goals and the reasons behind them, reminding everyone involved that student success is the focus. Colleagues can collaborate to find solutions that incorporate the ideas and address the concerns of all parties involved.

Advocating for Public Support of Reading Education

It is important for reading specialists to be aware of policies that affect literacy education at the local, state, and national levels. This includes awareness of school board, state government, and U.S. Department of Education policies. Attending local school board meetings and joining professional organizations that track impending legislation are two ways to assist with this goal. Reading specialists can share their knowledge with colleagues and community members and advocate for legislation and policies that support effective reading instruction. Additionally, they can interpret existing legislation for their colleagues and ensure that they understand the implications it has on their classroom instruction.

Reading specialists can also assist their school districts with writing grants and educational proposals that can positively impact literacy instruction. This may include proposals for funding that can be used to purchase new materials or hire additional reading specialists.

History of Reading Education in America

In colonial and early America, reading education focused on memorization. Students were expected to memorize the alphabet, syllables, words, verses, and poems. The poems and verses were recited in front of others for fluency practice.

In the 1800s, a more systematic approach to reading instruction was introduced. This included systematic phonics, sight word instruction, and reading across the content areas. McGuffey Readers were a series of leveled primers commonly used for reading instruction. In the late 1800s, the idea of reading for meaning began to be promoted.

In the early 1900s, the focus continued to be on reading for meaning and purpose. Explicit and systematic phonics instruction was common. In the mid-1900s, basal readers became commonplace in schools. Basal readers contained leveled stories that were followed by comprehension questions, with separate phonics skill and drill activities.

In the 1980s, whole language was promoted. Proponents believed children would learn to read by being immersed in reading and writing experiences rather than using explicit phonics instruction. By the mid-1990s, a balanced approach to literacy instruction was common. Balanced literacy includes a combination of explicit and systematic phonics instruction and immersion in authentic reading and writing experiences.

Evolution of Literacy Instruction over the Years

Beliefs about the best ways to teach reading have evolved over the years. It was once believed that children are passive receivers of knowledge, and memorization and skill and drill approaches to reading instruction were common. Later, theorists suggested that children are active learners who construct their own meaning through scaffolded problem-solving. Literacy instruction transitioned to focusing on reading and writing for authentic purposes.

Current research supports the idea that students are actively involved in the learning process. They should have opportunities to read and write for authentic purposes while also receiving systematic and explicit phonics instruction. Research also indicates that although children progress through typical stages of literacy development, learning is an individualized process. Differing prior knowledge and learning styles can affect the paths children take to becoming proficient readers and writers. Assessment is viewed as an important tool for helping ensure that learning is differentiated, and individual student needs are met. Additionally, research indicates that language and literacy development have social components, and students benefit from opportunities to interact and collaborate with others for a variety of authentic purposes.

Tenets of Behaviorism

The theory of behaviorism was shaped by several individuals, including Ivan Pavlov and B. F. Skinner. Popular in the early to mid-1900s, it centers around the belief that learners respond to external stimuli. If behaviors are reinforced, they will continue. Reinforcement may be positive, which occurs when stimuli are added after desired behaviors are demonstrated. Rewards and praise for completing assignments are examples of positive reinforcement. Reinforcement may also be negative, which occurs when stimuli are removed after desired behaviors are demonstrated. When teachers stop giving stern reminders to students after they begin their independent reading, negative reinforcement has occurred.

According to behaviorism, punishments are used to decrease undesirable behaviors. Taking away manipulatives from students who are misusing them is an example of using punishment to decrease undesirable behaviors.

Learning theory has evolved over time, and research now indicates that students are more actively involved in constructing meaning than suggested by behaviorism. Yet some tenets can still be applied to reading instruction. Teachers should be careful not to criticize or punish students for errors made during reading. Effort and use of reading strategies should be supported and encouraged.

Tenets of Cognitivism

Cognitivism became popular in the 1960s after the rise of behaviorism. Rather than believing that children are passive receivers of knowledge, cognitivism argued that there are many internal processes that affect learning. When students are confronted with new information, they attempt to make sense of it based on prior knowledge and other factors. Information that catches students' attention may proceed from sensory memory to short-term memory, where it must be processed and encoded to be transferred to long-term memory.

Cognitivism has many implications for reading instruction. Teachers should remember that learning to read is an active process. To facilitate memory transfer, students should have prior knowledge activated before reading. Attention must also be drawn to key information. This may be done using advance organizers, bolded text, or other cueing techniques. Information should also be broken into manageable chunks, and students should have opportunities to repeatedly practice new knowledge and skills. If too much information is presented at once, cognitive overload may occur. If students do not have opportunities to practice newly learned knowledge or skills, it may be forgotten. Teachers should ensure that they allow adequate opportunities for guided practice and feedback.

Piaget's Theory of Cognitive Development

Piaget's theory suggests that all children go through the same four stages of cognitive development, yet the rate at which they proceed through the stages may vary somewhat.

From birth until about two years of age, children are in the sensorimotor stage. Children in this stage explore the world around them using their senses, including grabbing and chewing objects. At first, children's behaviors are caused by reflexes. Gradually, they learn that their behaviors can influence their environments, and they begin experimenting with different behaviors. They learn object permanence, meaning they understand that things still exist even when they are not visible.

The preoperational stage lasts from age two until about age seven. In this stage, children begin thinking symbolically. They engage in symbolic play and begin using words to represent what they want. Children in this stage are egocentric and have trouble seeing other people's perspectives.

The concrete operational stage lasts from age seven until about age twelve. In this stage, children begin to think logically but may still struggle with abstract ideas. They begin becoming less egocentric.

In the formal operational stage, which begins around age 12 and continues into adulthood, people are capable of abstract and logical thoughts.

Applying Piaget's Theory of Cognitive Development to Reading Instruction

Young children in the sensorimotor stage of cognitive development benefit from exploring types of books designed for this age group. This includes board books and cloth books containing different textures and materials to manipulate. By exploring these books using their senses, children will enjoy their first reading experiences.

Children in the preoperational stage begin to think symbolically. The alphabetic principle can be explored in this stage. Children can also explore the purposes of punctuation marks and illustrations included in texts. They can explore using different types of texts to accomplish different purposes, such as writing letters to communicate with friends.

Children in the concrete operational stage begin to think logically. Students in this stage can explore literary elements and text structures. The can also analyze texts deeply and comprehend relationships like cause and effect.

By the formal operational stage, students should be reading and analyzing a variety of complex texts for personal and academic reasons.

Schema Theory

Schema theory suggests that when people learn new concepts, the new knowledge gets organized into units called schemata. These schemata include all of the information that is known about the concepts. For example, a young child's schema about cars might include knowing that they are used for transportation, they have four wheels and one steering wheel, and they are painted a variety of colors. These schemata are connected to one another when knowledge overlaps. For example, the child's schema about cars may be connected to his or her schema about motorcycles, which he or she knows also have wheels and are used for transportation. When encountering new information, people look to existing schemata to make sense of the new knowledge.

Schema theory has several implications for reading instruction. It demonstrates the importance of activating prior knowledge before reading. Students can be asked what they already know about the topics of new texts. They can also complete know, want, and learn (KWL) charts to identify what they already know and want to learn about the topics. Additionally, students can be encouraged to make text connections. This may include text-to-self, text-to-text, and text-to-world connections.

Assimilation and Accommodation in Piaget's Theory of Cognitive Development

According to Piaget, people have existing schemata, or units of knowledge, about concepts they have learned. They look to these existing schemata to make sense of new information they encounter.

Sometimes the newly encountered information fits within an existing schema and is added to it. For example, if a student has an existing schema about baseball and learns a new rule he or she did not previously know, he or she may add this new information to the schema. This is known as assimilation. However, sometimes the newly encountered information challenges the existing schema. If this occurs, the existing schema must be altered. For example, a student may have an existing schema about a historical figure based on readings he or she has done from one person's perspective. Based on these prior readings, he or she may view the figure as a hero. However, the student may then read a book about the figure written from a different perspective, which highlights the negative impacts of the figure's actions on others. This new knowledge may challenge the student's existing schema and cause him or her to alter it. This is known as accommodation.

Teachers should model and encourage evaluating texts and consider how they affirm or challenge existing beliefs.

Tenets of Lev Vygotsky's Social Development Theory

Lev Vygotsky played a leading role in the development of the constructivist learning theory. According to Vygotsky, children interact in social and cultural contexts. Through their social interactions with others in these contexts, cognitive development takes place. Therefore, social interaction plays a large role in learning. Teachers can consider how to incorporate social learning experiences into reading instruction. This may include shared and interactive reading and writing experiences, collaborative projects, reader's theater, and literature circles.

Vygotsky also suggested that learning takes place when students are engaged in activities in their zones of proximal development. These are activities that students are almost able to complete independently, but they require some scaffolding or collaboration. Vygotsky explained that scaffolding should be provided by others who have higher abilities in the tasks being completed. These individuals might be teachers, parents, or other classmates. Teachers can differentiate learning activities to ensure they are within students' zones of proximal development rather than being too easy or too difficult. For example, they can select books in students' instructional reading levels for guided reading groups. They can use assessments to determine how to differentiate instruction for each student.

Tenets of Constructivism

The constructivist theory was influenced by several people, including John Dewey, Jean Piaget, and Lev Vygotsky. Constructivism suggests that learning is an active process. Rather than passively receiving knowledge from their teachers, students actively construct their own meaning through learning experiences. Meaning may differ among individual students because they each have unique prior knowledge and experiences. According to constructivism, students learn by solving real-world problems; gathering, synthesizing, and evaluating information; and testing ideas.

Constructivism plays an important role in reading instruction. When analyzing texts, teachers can encourage students to draw upon prior knowledge, consider if any existing assumptions have been challenged, and share their unique understandings with others. Teachers can also encourage students to use reading to solve realistic problems through problem-based learning activities. They

- 94 -

can also give students some choices regarding the activities and methods used. Rather than directing all phases of assignments, teachers can instead use more collaborative approaches and provide scaffolding to students as needed.

Marie Clay's Literacy Processing Theory

Marie Clay's literacy processing theory has many underlying tenets. It suggests that all children approach learning to read with different background knowledge and experiences, which results in students taking different paths to becoming proficient readers and writers. It also suggests that reading and writing are complex and interrelated experiences, and children must read and write authentic texts to learn. Additionally, it suggests that learning to read and write are active processes, and children help create their own meanings.

Early childhood teachers should consider that all students have unique prior knowledge and experiences. They can assess students' skills and build upon their existing strengths. Additionally, if students are struggling with specific literacy skills, interventions can be implemented to address students' needs. Marie Clay promoted running records as one tool that can be used to identify strategy deficits and plan interventions. Teachers can also give students frequent opportunities to read and write authentic texts in addition to phonics instruction. Additionally, they can use these texts to model and teach concepts of print and decoding and comprehension strategies.

John Dewey's Contributions to Theories of Reading Instruction

John Dewey greatly influenced the constructivist theory of education. Dewey believed that people are active learners who learn by doing rather than passively receiving knowledge. He believed that valuable instructional time is wasted in schools by attempts to passively transmit knowledge. Additionally, he believed that for the teaching of symbolic concepts to be effective, students need opportunities to explore the symbols in context.

Dewey's beliefs have shaped the way reading instruction occurs today. Students are expected to be active learners who complete word work activities, problem-solve to decode and encode texts, and critically analyze a variety of text types. Children are commonly engaged in guided reading groups in which they must apply strategies to decode and comprehend real stories. They are also asked to construct their own meaning from texts by activating prior knowledge and making personal connections. When teaching symbolic relationships like the alphabetic principle, students are given opportunities to explore these relationships using real words and texts.

David Perkins' Theory of Learnable Intelligence

David Perkins theorized that humans have three types of intelligence. Neural intelligence is determined by genetics and cannot be changed. It is sometimes measured using IQ tests. Experiential intelligence is developed by the types of experiences one has. For example, a child who grows up in a big city may have knowledge of how to read subway maps and bus schedules. Having diverse experiences increases experiential intelligence. Reflective intelligence refers to a person's ability to problem-solve and reason. It also involves self-awareness and the use of metacognitive strategies. Unlike neural intelligence, experiential and reflective intelligence can be grown and developed over time.

Teachers can consider this theory when planning reading instruction. They can create literacy-rich environments using varied activities and types of texts. These varied experiences can help students develop experiential knowledge. Print, digital texts, and media can be used to help students experience things that are distant from their own communities. Teachers can also model and encourage the use of metacognitive and problem-solving strategies.

Howard Gardner's Theory of Multiple Intelligences

Howard Gardner theorized that there are multiple types of intelligences. According to his theory, people have different strengths and prefer to represent knowledge in different ways. He outlined eight different types of intelligences. Visual-spatial intelligence includes the ability to visualize things easily, such as charts and maps. Linguistic-verbal intelligence refers to strength in using language for reading, writing, listening, and speaking. Logical-mathematical intelligence refers to the ability to reason, solve problems, and recognize patterns, often with numbers. Bodily-kinesthetic intelligence refers to skilled coordination and movement. Musical intelligence refers to the ability to recognize rhythm, sound, beat, and other musical elements. Interpersonal intelligence refers to the ability to interact effectively with others. Intrapersonal intelligence refers to strong self-awareness. Naturalistic intelligence refers to a strong understanding of nature. Gardner explained that each person may demonstrate characteristics of multiple types of intelligence.

Teachers can consider Gardner's theory when planning instruction. They can use a multisensory approach to literacy instruction and also incorporate music, art, movement, problem-solving, collaboration, and other experiences. They can allow students choices in the topics they read and write about and allow them to present their learning in different ways.

Louise Rosenblatt's Transactional Theory of the Literary Work

Rosenblatt's Transactional Theory of the Literary Work suggests that reading involves a transaction between the reader and the text. Each reader brings unique prior knowledge and experiences to the reading experience. These differences affect how the text is interpreted and the meaning that is made. Different readers may make different meaning from the same texts. Therefore, there is no one fixed meaning in any text. Instead, the meaning is determined by the reader's transaction with the text.

This theory suggests that readers must be active participants in the reading process to make meaning. For example, they should be encouraged to activate prior knowledge, self-monitor understanding, and make connections before, during, and after reading. They should be encouraged to analyze texts deeply, and the close reading process may assist with this goal. Because different students may interpret texts differently, literature circles and other opportunities to discuss meaning can be beneficial. Students can be encouraged to share what prior experiences and text clues helped guide their interpretations.

Kenneth Goodman's Socio-Psycholinguistic Theory of Reading Instruction

Kenneth Goodman explained that reading involves the interaction between thinking and language. Beginning readers do not approach new texts already knowing how to read all of the words. Instead, they combine their thinking with available language clues to guess what the words say. By analyzing what readers guess and the errors that they make, teachers can gain insights into students' thinking and the cues they are using. They can identify if students are using or ignoring the graphophonic, semantic, and semantic cueing systems. Goodman also explained that teachers should observe students' reading behaviors to gain further insight into the reasons for their miscues. For example, teachers must determine if the errors are made due to lack of knowledge, such as not knowing how to decode certain consonant blends, or carelessness, such as reading too quickly.

The socio-psycholinguistic theory supports the use of running records to record reading behaviors and miscues. The results of the running records can be used to provide targeted instruction in using specific cueing systems.

Qualitative vs. Quantitative Research

Qualitative research is usually used to gather subjective information about people's opinions or understandings about things. Qualitative research can often be used to answer the questions what and why. Information may be gathered through focus groups, interviews, and observations. Researchers gather information in a neutral manner to ensure they do not influence the opinions of the subjects. Qualitative research could be used to determine reasons why teachers have abandoned a particular reading program, for example. This information could be used to revise the program to better meet teachers' needs and address concerns.

Quantitative research is used to gather numerical data that can be used to identify patterns and relationships. It can also be used to form generalizations and draw conclusions. For example, quantitative research could be used to identify if specific literacy interventions are leading to increased standardized test scores.

Characteristics of Valid Reading Research

With the ease with which people are able to post things on the Internet, abundant and often contradictory information about best practices in education can be found. Much of this information is not reliably tested. However, there are some characteristics that identify valid reading research, which teachers should use when making instructional decisions.

Reading research should be reliable. This means that other researchers should be able to replicate the research studies and get the same results. Research that relies on qualitative responses are more subjective and may be less likely to be replicated with the same results. This reliability should be taken into consideration when evaluating research. Reading research should also be valid, meaning the instruments should be designed to measure what they are supposed to measure. The research should also be credible. This means the research uses appropriate methodology, data collection, and analysis.

Sources of Valid Reading Research

There are many sources of valid reading research available. This research is sometimes available for free. Other times, paid subscriptions or enrollment in academic institutions is required to access the information.

The U.S. Department of Education provides information about reading research and statistics on its website. This includes information related to current reading programs, literacy progress, and more.

There are also many education-related journals that contain information about reading research. Peer-reviewed journals help ensure that the research is reliable and valid. Examples include *Language Arts*, published by the National Council of Teachers of English, and the *Harvard Educational Review*, published by the Harvard Graduate School of Education. Many of these journals are available online and are sometimes also available in print form.

There are also multiple databases containing reading research. One example is the Education Resources Information Center (ERIC). These databases are available online and are also commonly available in the libraries of educational institutions.

Myers-Briggs Type Indicator Personality Types

There are many different theories of personality that attempt to explain differences in the ways people perceive the world and interact with those around them. One common tool to assess personality type is the Myers-Briggs Type Indicator. Based on Carl Jung's personality theory, the Myers-Briggs Type Indicator outlines four different scales that affect personality.

The first scale ranges from introversion to extroversion. Introverts gain energy from time alone and quiet reflection, whereas extroverts gain energy from interacting with others. The second scale ranges from sensing to intuition. People on the sensing side of the scale learn from interacting with their senses, whereas people on the intuition side rely on instincts. The third scale ranges from thinking to feeling. People on the thinking side apply logic and questioning to make decisions, whereas people on the feeling side rely more on their emotions and values. The fourth scale ranges from judging to perceiving. People on the judging side of the scale prefer routine and order, whereas those on the perceiving side prefer a more laid-back approach.

Effect of Personality Types on Literacy Instruction

Teachers should consider the role that personality types play in how students learn and interact with others. Information observed about students' personality types can help teachers plan differentiated instruction that meets the needs of all students.

Classes typically include students on a range of the introversion-extroversion scale. Students who are more introverted may not enjoy reading instruction if they are continually asked to read aloud or perform in groups. However, students who are more extroverted may not enjoy reading instruction if only given opportunities to read independently and complete individual assignments.

Additionally, some students think logically and may instinctively turn to text evidence for support of answers. They may have more difficulties responding personally to texts. On the other hand, students who rely more on feeling may respond to texts emotionally yet need encouragement to support answers with evidence.

Personality type can also affect how students perceive classroom routines and procedures. Some students may prefer detailed routines for reading groups and centers, whereas others may prefer more laid-back approaches. Being aware of students' personalities can help teachers plan a mixture of activity types and give students the support they need to succeed in situations outside of their comfort zones.

Learning Behaviors

There are several learning behaviors applicable to all subject areas that support literacy learning. Some of these behaviors include following oral and written directions, interacting appropriately with other learners, displaying curiosity and asking questions, attempting to solve complex problems, reasoning, and focusing on learning tasks. These learning behaviors support literacy development by encouraging students to seek information to answer questions and solve realistic problems. They also support the collaboration needed to participate in shared problem-based learning activities and analysis of texts in literature circles. Focus on learning tasks also helps students develop reading stamina and the ability to complete literacy-related projects. Additionally, students who attempt to reason independently may find it easier to comprehend complex texts without assistance.

Age-appropriate reading, writing, listening, and speaking behaviors also help students convey and understand meaning. These behaviors include listening purposefully, organizing thoughts before writing and speaking, and monitoring understanding.

Bloom's Taxonomy

Benjamin Bloom outlined a hierarchy of skills in each of three learning domains, including the cognitive, affective, and psychomotor domains. The domain most often applied to classroom instruction is the cognitive domain. In the cognitive domain, skills are ranked in the following order: knowledge, comprehension, application, analysis, synthesis, and evaluation. Knowledge is the lowest-level skill, whereas evaluation is the highest.

Reading specialists and classroom teachers should consider Bloom's Taxonomy while designing instruction and assessments. Learning objectives should include specific verbs in the taxonomy that accurately describe what students are expected to be able to do at the end of instruction. Objectives should include skills in all levels of Bloom's Taxonomy, not just the lower levels. When reading nonfiction texts, for example, students may answer some basic recall questions. However, they may also be asked to evaluate authors' claims and support their evaluations with evidence. Higher-level thinking skills are important for close reading activities, and they help students more deeply comprehend their reading.

Components of Balanced Literacy Programs

Balanced literacy programs teach students a variety of reading skills and strategies that can be used to decode and comprehend texts. They include a mixture of systematic and explicit skills instruction and opportunities to read and write texts for authentic purposes.

Balanced literacy programs include instruction in phonological awareness. This is important because phonological awareness abilities are key indicators of future reading success. Systematic and explicit phonics instruction is also an important part of balanced literacy programs. Phonics skills are used to help students both decode and encode texts. Reading fluency is also modeled and practiced in balanced literacy programs. Additionally, vocabulary is another component. Students receive explicit instruction in using context and morphological clues to figure out the meanings of unknown words. They also build connections among meanings of related words. Comprehension strategies are also taught and practiced as part of balanced literacy programs.

Phonics-Based vs. Whole Language Approaches to Reading Instruction

Phonics-based reading programs use a bottom-up approach to instruction. Proponents of this approach believe that children learn best when instruction progresses from part to whole. They first teach children to identify letters and letter sounds. Next, they progress to teaching students to decode single words. Later, they decode sentences and longer texts.

Whole language reading programs use a top-down approach. Proponents of this approach believe children learn best from being immersed in authentic texts. They believe that by exploring these texts, children gradually learn the rules and patterns of language.

Teaching phonics helps students learn to decode and encode words and see relationships among spelling patterns. Rapid decoding also assists with fluency. However, if phonics skills are only taught in isolation, students miss out on opportunities to engage with texts and develop comprehension strategies. The whole language approach helps students understand how reading and writing are used to convey meaning for authentic purposes. However, some students may struggle with learning the rules and patterns needed to effectively decode and encode words. Research indicates that systematic and explicit phonics instruction and opportunities to read and write authentic texts are both important. Both should be components of balanced literacy programs.

Systems Used to Level Books

There are several different systems that are used to level books. Lexile measures consider both text complexity and word frequency to level books. Specialized assessments are used to determine students' Lexile levels, which can then be used to select appropriate books.

Irene Fountas and Gay Su Pinnell developed another system for leveling books based on their recommendations for guided reading groups. Their system, sometimes known as guided reading levels, considers several factors to assign book levels. These factors include word frequency, sentence complexity, vocabulary, and text features. Running records can help identify guided reading levels.

The Developmental Reading Assessment (DRA), also provides a system for leveling books. Students can take the DRA to determine their instructional reading levels. Results can then be used to select books using the DRA system.

Because there are many different leveling systems, conversion charts are available online to help teachers and parents identify book levels using their preferred systems.

Role of Flexible Groupings in Effective Reading Instruction

Flexible groupings are one way that teachers can differentiate instruction. When using flexible grouping, teachers strategically group students together to accomplish specific instructional goals. The groups may be large or small, and they vary depending on the activity. For example, a teacher may work with a small group of students who are all having difficulties with cause-and-effect relationships. The teacher is able to target instruction in this skill area to only the students who need extra practice. Guided reading groups are also flexible because students typically progress through instructional reading levels at different rates. Teachers can use both formal and informal assessment data to group students.

Flexible groupings have several benefits. They allow students to receive targeted instruction, often in small-group settings that allow for more teacher interaction. Students who have mastered these skills are able to work on other things, preventing them from becoming bored or frustrated. Additionally, students may feel more comfortable participating in small groups of their peers. Flexible groupings also mean that students will have opportunities to work with many other students throughout the year.

Considerations When Grouping Students for Instructional Purposes

When determining when and how to group students for instructional purposes, teachers should take many factors into consideration. They should consider what instructional goals they want to accomplish. These goals are often based upon specific learning objectives.

Once teachers know what goals they want to accomplish, they can consider what types of groupings to use. Possibilities include partner learning and small-, and large-group instruction. Teachers also need to consider the characteristics of the students in each group. For example, teachers may group students who need to practice specific skills together to target instruction. Other times, they may group students who have differing perspectives on topics to facilitate active discussion and sharing of viewpoints. These decisions should support the learning objectives. Teachers also need to consider what types of learning activities to use within the groups. Additionally, they need to consider what roles students will be assigned within their groups, if any. It is common for classrooms to use a variety of grouping arrangements throughout the year to accomplish different instructional goals.

Balancing Literacy Programs Using Literacy Centers

Literacy centers are important components of balanced literacy programs. They allow students to practice literacy skills on a regular basis while also allowing teachers time to work with small groups for guided reading instruction. Teachers typically create routines that allow students to rotate through some or all of the centers each day. Sometimes they are given choices over which centers to visit. Other times, teachers may direct students to proceed through the centers in predetermined orders for management purposes.

There are several common centers in literacy-rich classrooms. Independent reading centers include several texts of various genres for students to read by themselves, usually in relaxing and comfortable environments. Listening centers contain digital texts and headphones. Technology centers contain computers and/or tablets for literacy games, digital presentations, research, and more. Word work centers contain activities and manipulatives that allow students to explore how words and sentences are put together. Writing centers contain paper, dictionaries, and other materials students can use for writing. Partner reading centers provide places for students to read with one another. Early childhood classrooms may also contain sensory and dramatic play centers. Additionally, classrooms contain designated areas where teachers can meet with small groups for guided reading.

Classroom Management Strategies for Effective Guided Reading Groups

Guided reading groups are important components of balanced literacy programs because they allow students to receive differentiated, small-group instruction on a routine basis. However, they may be ineffective if frequent interruptions or classroom management issues occur. Clearly established and practiced routines can prevent these issues from occurring.

Students who are not working with their teachers in guided reading groups should be engaged in activities they are able to successfully complete either independently or with the help of their peers. If center rotations are being used, students should know in what order to proceed through the centers and what the expectations are for each rotation.

Additionally, routines should be in place for how to solve problems without interrupting the guided reading groups. There should be clear criteria in place for when the teachers can be interrupted, such as in the case of emergencies. Students should be taught how to independently access any materials they may need to complete their activities. Hand signals or sign-out sheets may be utilized to minimize interruptions when students need permission to leave the classroom. Students can also be taught to ask a set number of classmates for assistance with problems before asking their teachers.

Classroom Management Strategies for Effective Literacy Centers

It is important to establish clear routines and expectations for literacy centers at the beginning of each school year. If several literacy centers will be included, they should be gradually introduced a few at a time, especially for younger students. When introducing each center, teachers should discuss, and model expected center behavior. This includes explaining whether or not group work is allowed, how the materials should be properly used, and how to correctly complete the center activities. Each center's materials should be clearly labeled and be housed in designated locations.

Clear procedures should be in place for how students should rotate through the centers, minimizing confusion and overcrowding at each location. Countdown timers can be clearly displayed on projectors while students are working, providing warnings when it is time to clean up and rotate. Both auditory and visual clues can be provided to assist with transitions.

Teachers can also occasionally rotate center activities to allow students to practice newly learned skills and prevent boredom. However, teachers should model how to complete the new activities before asking students to do them independently during center time. This is especially important for young students who may not be able to read directions independently.

Record Keeping Strategies Useful in Literacy Instruction

Record keeping can assist teachers with assessing students' progress over time and differentiating instruction. Some teachers prefer to keep separate folders for each student. These folders may contain assessment data and work samples from throughout the year. Other teachers prefer to keep separate folders for each topic. For example, a teacher may have one guided reading folder that contains a list of students' current instructional reading levels and the skills that have been highlighted in each guided reading mini-lesson.

There are many types of records that may be useful. Copies of running records can be used to indicate students' growth in the use of reading strategies over time. Anecdotal records can provide information about observed reading behaviors and areas that need further instruction. Lists of students' reading levels and flexible grouping charts can assist teachers with planning guided reading groups. Writing portfolios can be used to demonstrate progress in writing over time, and they may be organized by genre, chronology, or other means. Dating each writing piece can assist teachers and students with observing growth over time.

Teachers may also keep records of literacy center schedules to ensure that students have opportunities to rotate through each center regularly.

Implementing Reading Programs with Fidelity

Implementing reading programs with fidelity means using them as the program developers intended. This includes following the intended pacing guides, incorporating all recommended instructional components, using the materials as intended, and more. Fidelity is necessary if reading programs are to be effectively evaluated after implementation. If not implemented with fidelity, unfavorable results may be due to causes unrelated to the quality of the programs. For example, students' comprehension scores may decline if teachers repeatedly skip the recommended comprehension components due to time constraints. Additionally, implementing the programs with fidelity helps ensure that students receive the research-based instruction promised by the programs. Presenting lessons out of sequence, omitting portions of instruction, and other changes may negatively affect the quality of instruction.

However, teachers sometimes have concerns with using reading programs exactly as intended. They may believe that some lessons are ineffective for their students, based on what they know about their students' prior knowledge and existing skills. Logistical issues, such as available time and resources, may also interfere with implementing programs with fidelity. When making instructional decisions, teachers and administrators must carefully weigh the program recommendations with their own beliefs about their students and best teaching practices.

Considerations When Selecting Reading Programs

There are numerous reading programs available, so educators should take several factors into consideration when determining which programs are best for their districts and schools. The selected programs should be based on reliable and valid research about how students learn best. Information should be provided about the research and educational philosophies the programs are based upon. Additionally, the selected programs should address all components of balanced literacy instruction, including phonological awareness, phonics, fluency, vocabulary development, and comprehension. Teacher guides should be available, with plans for systematic instruction using developmentally appropriate pacing guides. Frequent opportunities for explicit instruction, guided practice, and extension activities should be included in the instructional plans.

Reading programs should also contain plans and materials to help teachers differentiate instruction. The programs should offer support for struggling, on-level, and advanced readers as well as English language learners (ELLs). Leveled texts and tips for differentiating lesson plans may be included.

Additionally, selected reading programs should offer adequate professional development opportunities to help teachers use the programs successfully.

Evaluating Effectiveness of Reading Programs After They Have Been Implemented

Before selecting and implementing new reading programs, districts should consider the instructional and performance gaps they hope to address. By analyzing current performance data and identifying areas in need of improvement, districts can establish specific and measurable goals for their reading instruction. These goals can be used to select appropriate programs and to evaluate their effectiveness over time. By comparing data related to the goals from both before and after the new programs are implemented, districts can determine if the gaps are shrinking.

For example, a district may determine that many of its elementary students are not meeting grade-level expectations for reading fluency on standardized state tests. They may determine that one goal for their new reading program is to increase the percentage of elementary students who meet grade-level expectations for fluency by a certain amount over the next two years. They may then select a reading program that features daily fluency instruction and leveled texts for fluency practice. The district can then analyze the data from the same tests over the next few years to determine if the percentage of students who met grade-level expectations for fluency increased by the expected amount.

Increasing Positive Results When Implementing New Reading Programs

Strategic planning and ongoing support are both necessary for new program implementation to be successful. Rushing the process initially or tapering off support too soon can lead to both frustration and less-than-expected results.

It is important to have trusted reading specialists, administrators, or other educators who are well trained in the programs before they are introduced to teachers. These specialists should be available to address concerns and anxiety about the changes. These specialists should also share the research supporting the new programs and the district objectives they are designed to support.

Districts should also provide opportunities within teachers' workdays to learn how to use the new programs rather than requiring them to explore the programs on their own time. The trainings should be carefully planned to maximize the use of teachers' limited time. Teachers should have opportunities to observe other teachers who are already using the programs effectively.

It is also important to provide frequent support throughout the duration of each program rather than tapering off support after the initial training period. Educators should have ongoing opportunities to share successful strategies and discuss concerns with others. Support specialists should also be easily accessible when needed.

NES Practice Test

1. *Sea* and *see*, *fair* and *fare*, are called:
   - a. Homophones
   - b. Antonyms
   - c. Homographs
   - d. Twin words

2. Another name for a persuasive essay is:
   - a. Dynamic essay
   - b. Convincing essay
   - c. Argumentative essay
   - d. Position paper

3. A teacher is working with a group of third graders at the same reading level. Her goal is to improve reading fluency. She asks each child in turn to read a page from a book about mammal young. She asks the children to read with expression. She also reminds them they don't need to stop between each word; they should read as quickly as they comfortably can. She cautions them, however, not to read so quickly that they leave out or misread a word. The teacher knows the components of reading fluency are:
   - a. Speed, drama, and comprehension
   - b. Cohesion, rate, and prosody
   - c. Understanding, rate, and prosody
   - d. Rate, accuracy, and prosody

4. "Language load" refers to:
   - a. The basic vocabulary words a first grader has committed to memory
   - b. The number of unrecognizable words an English Language Learner encounters when reading a passage or listening to a teacher
   - c. The damage that carrying a pile of heavy books could cause to a child's physique
   - d. The number of different languages a person has mastered.

5. A syllable must contain:
   - a. A vowel
   - b. A consonant
   - c. Both a vowel and a consonant
   - d. A meaning

6. A third-grade teacher has several students reading above grade level. Most of the remaining students are reading at grade level. There are also a few students reading below grade level. She decides to experiment. Her hypothesis is that by giving the entire class a chapter book above grade level, high-level readers will be satisfied, grade-level readers will be challenged in a positive way, and students reading below grade level will be inspired to improve. Her method is most likely to:

    a. Succeed, producing students reading at an Instructional reading level. High-level readers will be happy to be given material appropriate to their reading level. Grade-level readers will challenge themselves to improve reading strategies in order to master the text. Because only a few of the students are reading below grade level, the other students, who feel happy and energized, will inspire the slower readers by modeling success.

    b. Succeed, producing students reading at an Independent reading level. High-level readers will independently help grade-level readers who will, in turn, independently help those below grade level.

    c. Fail, producing students at a Frustration reading level. Those reading below grade level are likely to give up entirely. Those reading at grade level are likely to get frustrated and form habits that will actually slow down their development.

    d. Fail, producing students reading at a Chaotic reading level. By nature, children are highly competitive. The teacher has not taken into consideration multiple learning styles. The children who are at grade level will either become bitter and angry at those whose reading level is above grade level or simply give up. The children reading below grade level will not be able to keep up and will in all likelihood act out their frustration or completely shut down.

7. Of the three tiers of words, the most important words for direct instruction are:

    a. Tier-one words
    b. Common words
    c. Tier-two words
    d. Words with Latin roots

8. At the beginning of each month, Mr. Yi has Jade read a page or two from a book she hasn't seen before. He notes the total number of words in the section, and also notes the number of times she leaves out or misreads a word. If Jade reads the passage with less than 3% error, Mr. Yi is satisfied that Jade is:

    a. Reading with full comprehension
    b. Probably bored and should try a more difficult book
    c. Reading at her Independent reading level
    d. Comfortable with the syntactical meaning

9. The purpose of corrective feedback is:

    a. To provide students with methods for explaining to the teacher or classmates what a passage was about

    b. To correct an error in reading a student has made, specifically clarifying where and how the error was made so that the student can avoid similar errors in the future

    c. To provide a mental framework that will help the student correctly organize new information

    d. To remind students that error is essential in order to truly understand and that it is not something to be ashamed of

10. Dr. Jenks is working with a group of high school students. They are about to read a science book about fossils. Before they begin, she writes the words *stromatolites, fossiliferous,* and *eocene* on the board. She explains the meaning of each word. These words are examples of:

    a. Academic words
    b. Alliteration
    c. Content-specific words
    d. Ionization

11. Which of the following best explains the importance prior knowledge brings to the act of reading?

    a. Prior knowledge is information the student gets through researching a topic prior to reading the text. A student who is well-prepared through such research is better able to decode a text and retain its meaning.
    b. Prior knowledge is knowledge the student brings from previous life or learning experiences to the act of reading. It is not possible for a student to fully comprehend new knowledge without first integrating it with prior knowledge.
    c. Prior knowledge is predictive. It motivates the student to look for contextual clues in the reading and predict what is likely to happen next.
    d. Prior knowledge is not important to any degree to the act of reading, because every text is self-contained and therefore seamless. Prior knowledge is irrelevant in this application.

12. A cloze test evaluates a student's:

    a. Reading fluency
    b. Understanding of context and vocabulary
    c. Phonemic skills
    d. Ability to apply the alphabetic principle to previously unknown material

13. Sight words are:

    a. Common words with irregular spelling
    b. Words that can easily be found on educational websites
    c. Any word that can be seen, including text words, words on signs, brochures, banners, and so forth
    d. There is no such thing; because oral language is learned before written language, all words are ultimately based on sound. The correct term is sound words and includes all words necessary to decode a particular text

14. *Phone, they, church.* The underlined letters in these words are examples of:

    a. Consonant blend
    b. Consonant shift
    c. Continental shift
    d. Consonant digraph

15. Phonemic awareness is a type of:

    a. Phonological awareness. Phonemic awareness is the ability to recognize sounds within words
    b. Phonics. It is a teaching technique whereby readers learn the relationship between letters and sounds
    c. Alphabetization. Unless a reader knows the alphabet, phonemic awareness is useless
    d. Syntactical awareness. Understanding the underlying structure of a sentence is key to understanding meaning

16. All members of a group of kindergarten students early in the year are able to chant the alphabet. The teacher is now teaching the students what the alphabet looks like in written form. The teacher points to a letter and the students vocalize the correspondent sound. Alternatively, the teacher vocalizes a phoneme and a student points to it on the alphabet chart. The teacher is using _____ in her instruction.

    a. Letter–sound correspondence
    b. Rote memorization
    c. Predictive analysis
    d. Segmentation

17. A fourth-grade teacher is preparing her students for a reading test in which a number of words have been replaced with blanks. The test will be multiple-choice; there are three possible answers given for each blank. The teacher instructs the children to read all the possible answers and cross out any answer that obviously doesn't fit. Next, the students should "plug in" the remaining choices and eliminate any that are grammatically incorrect or illogical. Finally, the student should consider contextual clues in order to select the best answer. This in an example of:

    a. Strategy instruction
    b. Diagnostic instruction
    c. Skills instruction
    d. Multiple-choice instruction

18. The term "common words" means:

    a. One-syllable words with fewer than three letters. Some examples are it, an, a, I, go, to, and in. They are the first words an emergent writer learns
    b. One-syllable words with fewer than five letters. Some examples include sing, goes, sit, rock, walk, and took
    c. Words that are ordinary or unexceptional; because they tend to flatten a piece of writing, they should be avoided
    d. Familiar, frequently used words that do not need to be taught beyond primary grades

19. Which is greater, the number of English phonemes or the number of letters in the alphabet?

    a. The number of letters in the alphabet, because they can be combined to create phonemes
    b. The number of phonemes. A phoneme is the smallest measure of language sound
    c. They are identical; each letter "owns" a correspondent sound
    d. Neither. Phonemes and alphabet letters are completely unrelated

20. *Train, brain, spring.* The underlined letters are examples of:

    a. Consonant digraph
    b. Consonant blend
    c. Consonant shift
    d. Continental shift

21. It is the beginning of the school year. To determine which second-grade students might need support, the reading teacher wants to identify those who are reading below grade level. She works with students one at a time. She gives each child a book at a second-grade reading level and asks the child to read out loud for two minutes. Children who will need reading support are those who read:

    a. Fewer than 100 words in the time given
    b. Fewer than 200 words in the time given
    c. More than 75 words in the time given
    d. The entire book in the time given

22. The most effective strategy for decoding sight words is:

    a. Segmenting sight words into syllables. Beginning readers are understandably nervous when encountering a long word that isn't familiar. Blocking off all but a single syllable at a time renders a word manageable and allows the reader a sense of control over the act of reading
    b. Word families. By grouping the sight word with similar words, patterns emerge
    c. A phonemic approach. When students understand the connection between individual words and their sounds, they will be able to sound out any sight word they encounter
    d. None; sight words cannot be decoded. Readers must learn to recognize these words as wholes on sight

23. Which of the following choices will be most important when designing a reading activity or lesson for students?

    a. Selecting a text
    b. Determining the number of students participating
    c. Analyzing the point in the school year at which the lesson is given
    d. Determining a purpose for instruction

24. "Decoding" is also called:

    a. Remediation
    b. Deciphering
    c. Alphabetic principle
    d. Deconstruction

25. Which text(s) are likely to foster the greatest enthusiasm for reading and literature among students?

    a. Free choice of reading texts, provided that students complete class assignments, projects, and discussions
    b. An all-in-one textbook that includes all reading material for the year, study guides, and sample test questions
    c. A variety of texts, including books, magazines, newspapers, stories from oral traditions, poetry, music, and films
    d. A small selection of current best-selling books for children, some of which the children may already have read and liked

26. Phonological awareness activities are:

    a. Oral
    b. Visual
    c. Both A and B
    d. Semantically based

27. A student is able to apply strategies to comprehend the meanings of unfamiliar words; can supply definitions for words with several meanings such as *crucial, criticism,* and *witness*; and is able to reflect on her background knowledge in order to decipher a word's meaning. These features of effective reading belong to which category?

    a. Word recognition
    b. Vocabulary
    c. Content
    d. Comprehension

28. A reading teacher is assessing an eighth grader to determine her reading level. Timed at a minute, the student reads with 93% accuracy. She misreads an average of seven words out of 100. What is her reading level?

    a. She is reading at a Frustration level
    b. She is reading at an Excellence level
    c. She is reading at an Instructional level
    d. She is reading at an Independent level

29. When should students learn how to decode?

    a. Decoding is the most basic and essential strategy to becoming a successful reader. It should be introduced to kindergartners during the first two weeks of school
    b. Decoding is not a teachable skill. It is an unconscious act and is natural to all learners
    c. Decoding should be taught only after children have mastered every letter–sound relationship as well as every consonant digraph and consonant blend. They should also be able to recognize and say the 40 phonemes common to English words and be able to recognize at least a dozen of the most common sight words
    d. Decoding depends on an understanding of letter–sound relationships. As soon as a child understands enough letters and their correspondent sounds to read a few words, decoding should be introduced

30. *Since, whether,* and *accordingly* are examples of which type of signal words?

    a. Common, or basic, signal words
    b. Compare/contrast words
    c. Cause–effect words
    d. Temporal sequencing words

31. A class is reading *The Heart Is a Lonely Hunter*. The teacher asks students to write a short paper explaining the story's resolution. She is asking them to locate and discuss the story's:

    a. Outcome
    b. Highest or most dramatic moment
    c. Plot
    d. Lowest point

32. A student encounters a multisyllabic word. She's not sure if she's seen it before. What should she do first? What should she do next?

    a. Locate familiar word parts, then locate the consonants
    b. Locate the consonants, then locate the vowels
    c. Locate the vowels, then locate familiar word parts
    d. Look it up in the dictionary, then write down the meaning

The following passage pertains to the following questions 33 - 36:

The kindergarten teacher is concerned about three of her students. While they are enthusiastic about writing, they do not always recognize letters, confusing b, d, and p, or e and o. They do, however, know which sounds go with certain letters when they are orally drilled. When they write, they appear to be attempting letter–sound associations.

"Now I'm writing *M*," the teacher heard one boy say as he scripted a large *N* in the upper right corner of his paper. He studied it for a moment and added, "Nope, it needs another leg." The student then wrote an *I* beside the *N*. "There," he said. "Now you are an *M*. I can write the word, 'man,' because now I have *M*." The child then moved to the lower left corner of the paper. "M-A-N," he said to himself, slowly pronouncing each sound. "I already have that *M*. Here is where the rest of the word goes." He turned the paper sideways and wrote *N*.

The second child sang to herself as she gripped the crayon and scribbled lines here and there on her paper. Some of the lines resembled letters, but few actually were. Others were scribbles. As she "wrote," she seemed to be making up a story and seemed to believe she was writing the story down.

The third child didn't vocalize at all while he worked. He gripped the paper and carefully wrote the same letter over and over and over. Sometimes the letter was large, sometimes tiny. He turned the paper in every direction so that sometimes the letter was sideways or upside down. Sometimes he flipped it backward. "What are you writing?" the teacher asked him. "My name," the child told her. The teacher then realized the letter was, indeed, the first letter of his name. She gently told him he had done a fine job of writing the first letter of his name. Did he want her to help him write the rest of it? "Nope," he cheerfully told her, "it's all here." He pointed at one of the letters and "read" his full name. He pointed at another letter and again seemed to believe it represented all the sounds of his name.

33. The kindergarten teacher isn't certain if these children are exhibiting signs of a reading disability or other special needs. What should the teacher do?

    a. Nothing. These children are simply at an early stage in the reading/writing process
    b. Nothing. She doesn't want to have to tell the parents that their children are sub-par in terms of intelligence. They are perfectly nice children and can contribute to society in other ways. She resolves to give them extra attention in other areas to help them build confidence
    c. She should recommend that the parents take the children to be tested for a number of reading disorders, including dyslexia
    d. She should arrange a meeting between herself, the school psychologist, and the reading specialist to discuss the matter and resolve it using a three-pronged approach

34. In the above example, the emergent writers are demonstrating their understanding that letters symbolize predictable sounds, that words begin with an initial sound/letter, and that by "writing," they are empowering themselves by offering a reader access to their thoughts and ideas. The next three stages the emergent writers will pass through in order will most likely be:

   a. Scripting the end-sound to a word (KT=cat); leaving space between words; writing from the top left to the top right of the page, and from top to bottom
   b. Scripting the end-sound to a word (KT=cat); writing from the top left to the top right of the page, and from top to bottom; separating the words from one another with a space between
   c. Leaving space between the initial letters that represent words; writing from the top left to the top right of the page, and from top to bottom; scripting the final sound of each word as well as the initial sound (KT=cat)
   d. Drawing a picture beside each of the initial sounds to represent the entire word; scripting the end-sound to a word (KT=cat); scripting the interior sounds that compose the entire word (KAT=cat)

35. The teacher might best encourage the three students in the above example by:

   a. Suggesting they write an entire book rather than just a single page. This will build confidence, teach them sequencing, and encourage the young writers to delve deeper into their ideas.
   b. Ask the students to read their stories to her. Suggest they visit other children in the class and read to each of them.
   c. Contact the local newspaper and invite a reporter to visit her class and write a story about her emergent writers. In this way, they are sure to see themselves as "real writers" and will more fully apply themselves to the task.
   d. Invite all the parents to visit the class the following week. This will give all classmates, regardless of where they are on the learning spectrum, time to memorize their stories. The children will be very excited and will begin to see themselves as "real writers."

36. At what point should the kindergarten teacher in the above example offer the three children picture books and ask them to read to her?

   a. When the three children are all able to script initial sounds, end sounds, and interior sounds they are ready to decode words. She should make her request at this point
   b. As each child reaches the stage in which he or she can script initial sounds, end sounds, and interior sounds, the teacher should ask only that child to read to her
   c. As each child reaches the stage in which he habitually writes from the top to the bottom of the page, moving left to right, the time has come. Books are intended to be read in this way, and until a child has had the experience of writing in the same manner, he won't be able to make sense of the words
   d. The teacher should encourage all students to "read" picture books from the first day of school. Talking about the pictures from page to page gives young readers the idea that books are arranged sequentially. Pictures also offer narrative coherence and contextual clues. Emergent readers who are encouraged to enjoy books will more readily embrace the act of reading. Holding a book and turning pages gives young readers a familiarity with them

37. Which of the following statements regarding the acquisition of language is false?

    a. Young children often have the ability to comprehend written language just as early as they can comprehend or reproduce oral language when given appropriate instruction
    b. Oral language typically develops before a child understands the relationship between spoken and written word
    c. Most young children are first exposed to written language when an adult reads aloud
    d. A child's ability to speak, read, and write depends on a variety of physiological factors, as well as environmental factors

38. A teacher is teaching students analogizing. She is teaching them to:

    a. Identify and use metaphors
    b. Identify and use similes
    c. Identify and use groups of letters that occur in a word family
    d. Identify and use figures of speech

39. A reading teacher is working with a student who has just moved to Texas from Korea. The child knows very few words in English. The teacher offers her a picture book of Korean folk tales. Using words and gestures, the teacher asks her to "read" one folk tale. The child "reads" the familiar tale in Korean. The teacher then writes key English words on the board and asks the child to find those words in the book. When the child finds the words, they read them together. This strategy is:

    a. Useful. The child will feel more confident because the story is already familiar. She will also feel that the lesson is a conversation of sorts, and that she is communicating successfully. She will be motivated to learn the English words because they are meaningful and highly charged
    b. Useful. The teacher is learning as much as the child is. The teacher is learning about Korean culture and language, and she can apply this knowledge when teaching future Korean students
    c. Not very useful. The child needs to be exposed to as much American culture as possible. Encouraging her to remember her own culture will make her sad and will limit her curiosity about her new home
    d. Not very useful. The first things the child should learn are the letters of the alphabet and associative sounds. Only then can she begin to decipher an unfamiliar language

40. The teacher in the previous question was using what kind of load?

    a. Language load
    b. Cognitive load
    c. Bilingual load
    d. Cultural load

41. Using brain imaging, researchers have discovered that dyslexic readers use the _____ side(s) of their brains, while non-dyslexic readers use the _____ side(s) of their brains.

    a. Left; right
    b. Right; left
    c. Right and left; left
    d. Right; left and right

42. A fifth grader has prepared a report on reptiles, which is something he knows a great deal about. He rereads his report and decides to make a number of changes. He moves a sentence from the top to the last paragraph. He crosses out several words and replaces them with more specific words. He circles key information and draws an arrow to show another place the information could logically be placed. He is engaged in:

a. Editing
b. Revising
c. First editing, then revising
d. Reviewing

43. *Bi, re,* and *un* are:

a. Suffixes, appearing at the beginning of base words to change their meaning
b. Suffixes, appearing at the end of base words to enhance their meaning
c. Prefixes, appearing at the beginning of base words to emphasize their meaning
d. Prefixes, appearing at the beginning of base words to change their meanings

44. Examples of CVC words include:

a. Add, pad, mad
b. Cat, tack, act
c. Elephant, piano, examine
d. Dog, sit, leg

45. A teacher is working with a student who is struggling with reading. The teacher gives him a story with key words missing:

> The boy wanted to take the dog for a walk. The boy opened the door. The ____ ran out. The ___ looked for the dog. When he found the dog, he was very _____.

The student is able to fill in the blanks by considering:

a. Syntax. Oftentimes, word order gives enough clues that a reader can predict what happens next.
b. Pretext. By previewing the story, the student can deduce the missing words.
c. Context. By considering the other words in the story, the student can determine the missing words.
d. Sequencing. By putting the ideas in logical order, the student can determine the missing words.

46. The following is/are (an) element(s) of metacognition:

a. A reader's awareness of herself as a learner
b. A reader's understanding of a variety of reading strategies and how to apply them to comprehend a text
c. A reader who is conscious about remembering what has been read
d. All of the above

47. Collaborative Strategic Reading (CSR) is a teaching technique that depends on two teaching practices. These practices are:

a. Cooperative learning and reading comprehension
b. Cooperative reading and metacognition
c. Reading comprehension and metacognition
d. Cooperative learning and metacognition

48. Context clues are useful in:
   a. Predicting future action
   b. Understanding the meaning of words that are not familiar
   c. Understanding character motivation
   d. Reflecting on a text's theme

49. A teacher has a child who does not volunteer in class. When the teacher asks the student a question the student can answer, she does so with as few words as possible. The teacher isn't sure how to best help the child. She should:
   a. Leave the child alone. She is clearly very shy and will be embarrassed by having attention drawn to her. She is learning in her own way.
   b. Ask two or three highly social children to include this girl in their activities. She is shy, and she probably won't approach them on her own.
   c. Observe the child over the course of a week or two. Draw her into conversation and determine if her vocabulary is limited, if she displays emotional problems, or if her reticence could have another cause. Note how the child interacts with others in the class. Does she ever initiate conversation? If another child initiates, does she respond?
   d. Refer her to the school counselor immediately. It is clear the child is suffering from either a low IQ or serious problems at home.

50. For their monthly project, a group of students can choose to read and respond to one book on a list supplied by their teacher. The books are grouped according to genre. Most students choose books listed under the genre that is described as "modern-day stories that are not true, but seem as though they could really happen." Which genre did most of the students choose from?
   a. Historical fiction
   b. Autobiography
   c. Realistic fiction
   d. Fantasy

51. A high school class reads an essay about the possible effects of sexual activity on teens. The author's position is very clear: She believes young people should avoid sex because they aren't mature enough to take the necessary steps to remain safe. The author cites facts, research studies, and statistics to strengthen her position. This type of writing is called:
   a. Expository
   b. Narrative
   c. Persuasive
   d. Didactic

52. A reading teacher feels that some of his strategies aren't effective. He has asked a specialist to observe him and make suggestions as to how he can improve. The reading specialist should suggest that first:

    a. The teacher set up a video camera and record several sessions with different students for the specialist to review. The presence of an observer changes the outcome; if the specialist is in the room, it will negatively affect the students' ability to read
    b. The teacher reflects on his strategies himself. Which seem to work? Which don't? Can the teacher figure out why? It's always best to encourage teachers to find their own solutions so that they can handle future issues themselves
    c. They meet to discuss areas the teacher is most concerned about and decide on the teacher's goals
    d. The specialist should arrive unannounced to observe the teacher interacting with students. This will prevent the teacher from unconsciously over-preparing

53. A kindergarten teacher pronounces a series of word pairs for her students. The students repeat the pairs. Some of the pairs rhyme (*see/bee*) and some of the pairs share initial sounds but do not rhyme (*sit, sun*). The students help her separate the word pairs into pairs that rhyme and pairs that do not. Once the students are able to distinguish between two words that rhyme and two words that do not, the teacher says a word and asks them to provide a rhyme. When she says *cat* a child responds with *fat*. When she says *sing* a child offers *thing*. How does this strictly oral activity contribute to the children's ability to read?

    a. It doesn't. Oral activities must have a written component to be useful to emergent readers
    b. It is helpful in that it demonstrates how different sounds are made with different letters
    c. It actually discourages children from reading. By emphasizing orality over literacy, the teacher is suggesting to the children that reading is not an important skill
    d. Being able to identify rhyme is an important element of phonological awareness

54. Syllable types include:

    a. Closed, open, silent e, vowel team, vowel-r, and consonant-le
    b. Closed, open, silent, double-vowel, r, and le
    c. Closed, midway, open, emphasized, prefixed, and suffixed
    d. Stressed, unstressed, and silent

55. An eighth-grade student is able to decode most words fluently and has a borderline/acceptable vocabulary, but his reading comprehension is quite low. He can be helped with instructional focus on:

    a. Strategies to increase comprehension and to build vocabulary
    b. Strategies to increase comprehension and to be able to identify correct syntactical usage
    c. Strategies to improve his understanding of both content and context
    d. Strategies to build vocabulary and to improve his understanding of both content and context

56. Reading comprehension and vocabulary can best be assessed:

a. With brief interviews and tests every two months to determine how much learning has taken place. Students learn in spurts, and in-depth assessments of comprehension and vocabulary are a waste of time

b. Through a combination of standardized testing, informal teacher observations, attention to grades, objective-linked assessments, and systematized charting of data over time

c. By giving students weekly self-assessment rubrics to keep them constantly aware of and invested in their own progress

d. By having students retell a story or summarize the content of an informational piece of writing. The degree to which the material was comprehended, and the richness or paucity of vocabulary used in such work, provides efficient and thorough assessment

57. An ORF is:

a. An Oral Reading Fluency assessment

b. An Occasional Reading Function assessment

c. An Oscar Reynolds Feinstein assessment

d. An Overt Reading Failure assessment

58. Round-robin reading refers to the practice of allowing children to take turns reading portions of a text aloud to the rest of the group during class. Which of the following statements is <u>least</u> true about this practice?

a. Students have the chance to practice reading aloud with this strategy

b. This practice is ineffective in its use of time, leaving students who are not reading aloud to become bored or daydream

c. Round-robin reading lacks the creativity or engaging qualities that will interest students in building literacy skills

d. This practice helps students feel comfortable with reading aloud due to continuous practice and encouragement from the teacher and peers

59. Word-recognition ability is:

a. Equally important to all readers

b. Used only by fluent readers

c. Another term for "word attack"

d. Especially important to English Language Learners and students with reading disabilities

60. Research indicates that developing oral language proficiency in emergent readers is important because:

a. Proficiency with oral language enhances students' phonemic awareness and increases vocabulary

b. The more verbally expressive emergent readers are, the more confident they become. Such students will embrace both Academic and Independent reading levels

c. It encourages curiosity about others. With strong oral language skills, students begin to question the world around them. The more they ask, the richer their background knowledge

d. It demonstrates to students that their ideas are important and worth sharing

61. In preparation for writing a paper, a high school class has been instructed to skim a number of Internet and print documents. They are being asked to:

a. Read the documents several times, skimming to a deeper level of understanding each time
b. Read the documents quickly, looking for those that offer the most basic, general information
c. Read the documents quickly, looking for key words in order to gather the basic premise of each
d. Read the documents carefully, looking for those that offer the most in-depth information

62. The students in the above question are most likely preparing to write a(n) _____ essay:

a. Personal
b. Expository
c. Literary
d. Narrative

A teacher has given the first paragraph of an essay to her students to analyze and discuss. Read the paragraph and answer the following questions 63-65:

> Americans have struggled with cigarettes far too long. Until now, it has been a personal choice to smoke (or not), but the time for change is rapidly approaching. Local legislation has already begun for schools, restaurants, arenas, and other public places to be smoke-free. Years ago cigarette smoking was presented by the media as being fashionable, even sexy. In magazines, movies, and later in television, celebrities would indulge themselves with a smoke and even be paid to endorse a brand. As recently as 1975, it was common for talk show hosts like Tom Snyder and Johnny Carson to keep a cigarette burning. Cigarette smoking in America has persisted in spite of frightening concerns like lung cancer and emphysema. Over the years, the tobacco industry has sought to diffuse strong evidence that smoking is harmful. However, the myth of "safe cigarettes," questions about nicotine addiction, and denials about the dangers of secondhand smoke have proven to be propaganda and lies.

63. This is a(n) _____ essay:

a. Compare/contrast
b. Persuasive
c. Narrative
d. Analytic

64. The thesis statement is:

a. However, the myth of "safe cigarettes," questions about nicotine addiction, and denials about the dangers of secondhand smoke have proven to be propaganda and lies
b. Americans have struggled with cigarettes far too long
c. Until now, it has been a personal choice to smoke (or not), but the time for change is rapidly approaching
d. In magazines, movies, and later in television, celebrities would indulge themselves with a smoke and even be paid to endorse a brand

65. The next three paragraphs in the essay will most likely address:

   a. Smoking as a personal choice, changes in local legislation, and how fashionable smoking once was
   b. How fashionable smoking once was, talk show hosts smoking on air, the myth of "safe cigarettes"
   c. Propaganda and lies, the myth of "safe cigarettes," and how long Americans have struggled with cigarettes
   d. The myth of "safe cigarettes," questions about nicotine addiction, and the dangers of secondhand smoke

66. The teacher and her students brainstorm a list of talents, skills, and specialized knowledge belonging to members of the class. Some of the items on the list include how to make a soufflé, how to juggle, and how to teach a dog to do tricks. One student knows a great deal about spiders, and another about motorcycles. She asks each student to write an essay about something he or she is good at or knows a great deal about. What kind of essay is she asking the students to produce?

   a. Cause and effect
   b. Compare/contrast
   c. Example
   d. Argumentative

67. *Caret, carrot, to, two and too* share something in common. They:

   a. Are nouns
   b. Are monosyllabic
   c. Are homophones
   d. Represent things in nature

Questions 68 – 70 pertain to the following paragraph:

   A class will visit an assisted living facility to interview residents about their lives. Each group of three has selected a theme such as love, work, or personal accomplishment and written several questions around that theme. Next each. group practices interviewing one another. The teacher then asks all the students to discuss the questions that caused them to respond most thoughtfully, as well as those they were less inspired by. The students decided the questions that were easiest to respond to asked for very specific information; for example, one inspiring question was, "Please tell me about something you learned to do as a child that affected the direction of your life." Those that were uninspiring were too broad, for example, "Please tell me about your happiest memory."

68. After they interview the residents, each group of three students will work together to write a piece about the resident. This kind of approach is called:

   a. Collaborative learning
   b. Companion learning
   c. Bonded learning
   d. Group learning

69. The genre the teacher expects is:

    a. Memoir
    b. Historical fiction
    c. Biography
    d. Autobiography

70. The teacher wants the students to apply what they've learned across content areas. Which of the following strategies would be most effective?

    a. Students will interview a family member, asking the same questions
    b. Students will write a personal piece in which they address the same questions
    c. Students will do online research about the cultural, economic, or political events that were occurring during the specific time about which they've written
    d. Students pretend to be the interviewee and rewrite the piece from a first person point of view

The following passage pertains to questions 71 – 73:

> A seventh-grade teacher asks the reading teacher to suggest a lesson students will find simultaneously challenging and fun. The reading teacher suggests the class read fairy tales from both Hans Christian Anderson and the Brothers Grimm and have a rapid-paced, energetic discussion about the many similarities and differences between the two while the teacher lists them on the board.

71. The individual strategies the students will employ are:

    a. Collaborative learning and genre
    b. Brainstorming and a compare/contrast strategy
    c. Collaborative learning and brainstorming
    d. Analyzing and genre

72. The lesson is asking the students to consider two different:

    a. Learning styles
    b. Genres
    c. Writing styles
    d. Reading styles

73. The primary benefit of this exercise is that it promotes students':

    a. Vocabulary
    b. Comprehension
    c. Fluency
    d. Word identification

74. The students enjoyed the assignment so much that the teacher suggested they select one fairy tale and modernize it without changing the basic structure. Evil kings and queens could become corrupt politicians; pumpkins could turn into Hummers; and romantic princes might reveal themselves as rock stars. The teacher believes this assignment will most effectively demonstrate to the students:

    a. The importance of setting to meaning
    b. The importance of characters to meaning
    c. The importance of culture to meaning
    d. The importance of creativity to meaning

75. The first-grade teacher wants her class to understand that stories have a certain order. She reads them a story, then orally reviews with them how each event that happened in the story caused the next event to happen. To reinforce the lesson the teacher should:

   a. Give each child a piece of drawing paper that has been folded in half and then again, creating four boxes, along with a piece that has not been folded. The teacher should then ask the students to draw a cartoon about the story. Each of the first four boxes will show the events in order. The second page is to show how the story ends

   b. Give each child a piece of drawing paper and ask the students to draw the most important scene

   c. Give each child a piece of drawing paper and ask the students to draw the story's beginning on the front of the page and ending on the back

   d. Give each child a piece of drawing paper that has been folded in half and then again, creating four boxes, along with a piece that has not been folded. The teacher should then ask the students to draw a cartoon about anything they want. She reminds them to put their story cartoons in proper order

76. A ninth grade class is reading a 14-line poem in iambic pentameter. There are three stanzas of four lines each, and a two-line couplet at the end. Words at the end of each line rhyme with another word in the same stanza. The class is reading a:

   a. Sonnet
   b. Villanelle
   c. Sestina
   d. Limerick

77. A teacher is working with a group of English Language Learners. She asks them to take two pieces of paper. At the top of the first paper they are to write *SAME*, at the top of the other, *DIFFERENT*. Each child will consider what his native country and the United States have in common, and what distinct features each country possesses. The children are using which method in organizing their ideas?

   a. Hunt and peck
   b. Consider and persuade
   c. Evaluate and contrast
   d. Compare and contrast

78. Which student is most likely to need referral to a reading specialist for assessment, special instruction, or intervention?

   a. Annabel: a 2nd-grade student who tends to skip over words or phrases when she reads, affecting her comprehension of the text

   b. Cliff: a kindergarten student who is already reading simple chapter books with his parents at home or in class

   c. Noelle: a 1st-grader who avoids any activity in which she must read, both aloud and silently, preferring to ask an adult to read the text for her first

   d. Barrett: a 3rd-grader who often confuses the sounds of certain letters, such as /b/ and /d/ or /v/ and /u

- 121 -

79. Which assessment will determine a student's ability to identify initial, medial, blended, final, segmented, and manipulated 'units'?

    a. Phonological awareness assessment
    b. High-frequency word assessment
    c. Reading fluency assessment
    d. Comprehension quick-check

80. A third grader knows he needs to write from left to right and from top to bottom on the page. He knows what sounds are associated with specific letters. He can recognize individual letters and can hear word families. He correctly identifies prefixes, suffixes, and homonyms, and his reading comprehension is very good. However, when he is asked to write, he becomes very upset. He has trouble holding a pencil, his letters are very primitively executed, and his written work is not legible. He most likely has:

    a. Dysgraphia
    b. Dyslexia
    c. Dyspraxia
    d. Nonverbal learning disorder

81. The phrase "Pretty as a picture" is *best* described as a:

    a. Metaphor
    b. Cliché
    c. Simile
    d. Figure of speech

82. A fourth-grade teacher had her students write haiku in order to promote the students' _____.

    a. Reading comprehension
    b. Vocabulary
    c. Word identification skills
    d. Confidence

83. A second-grade teacher wants to help her students enrich their vocabulary. She's noticed that their writing journals are filled with serviceable but unexciting verbs such as "said" and "went," and general rather than specific nouns. The most effective lesson would involve:

    a. Suggesting students use a thesaurus to substitute more unusual words for common ones
    b. Suggesting students add an adjective to each noun
    c. Brainstorming a list of verbs that mean ways of talking or ways of going, then adding them to the word wall along with some nouns that specify common topics
    d. Suggesting students look up the meanings of boring words and consider another way to express them

84. Activating prior knowledge, shared reading, and using graphic organizers are all examples of what type of instructional concept?

    a. Modeling
    b. Scaffolding
    c. Assessing
    d. Inspiring

85. Examples of onomatopoeia are:

    a. Sink, drink, mink, link
    b. Their, there, they're
    c. Drip, chirp, splash, giggle
    d. *Think, in, thin, ink*

86. "Code knowledge" facilitates reading fluency because:

    a. It brings the entirety of the student's previous experience to bear on decoding a text
    b. It offers a framework for organizing new information by assigning code words to sets of ideas
    c. There is no such thing as "code knowledge." The correct term is "core knowledge"
    d. It offers a systematic approach to untangling the wide variety of vowel sounds when an unfamiliar word is encountered

87. The purpose of "targeted instruction" is to:

    a. Deliver instructions that are precise, clear, and direct so that students understand exactly what is expected
    b. Accurately rank a group of learners from low achievers to high achievers so that the teacher knows from the beginning of the school year which students have less ability and will therefore need support
    c. Teach students how to take information from a text and reorganize it into bulleted lists
    d. Assess and target areas needing improvement as well as areas of greatest strength for each student to ensure that all members of a class are receiving instruction tailored to their specific needs

88. Components of "explicit instruction" include:

    a. Clarifying the goal, modeling strategies, and offering explanations geared to a student's level of understanding
    b. Determining the goal, offering strategies, and asking questions designed to ascertain whether understanding has been reached
    c. Reassessing the goal, developing strategies, and determining whether further reassessing of the goal is required
    d. Objectifying the goal, assessing strategies, and offering explanations geared toward a student's level of understanding.

89. A teacher has challenged a student with a book about Antarctica that is just beyond the high end of the student's Instructional level. The teacher points out that the student already knows quite a bit about penguins because the class studied them earlier in the year. He reminds the student that she's recently seen a television show about the seals that also live in Antarctic waters. The teacher gives the student a list of words she's likely to find in the text, and they discuss what those words might mean. The student begins to read, but stops to ask the teacher what *circumpolar* means. The teacher is also unfamiliar with the word, but reminds her that *circum* is a prefix. The student recalls that it means "about or around" and deduces that circumpolar most likely refers to something found around or in a polar region. This instructional approach is called:

    a. Modular instruction
    b. Scaffolding
    c. Linking
    d. Transmutation

90. Which choice is <u>not</u> a cueing system used to understand unfamiliar words?

    a. Syntactic
    b. Semantic
    c. Graphophonic
    d. Auditory

91. An understanding of the meanings of prefixes and suffixes such as *dis, mis, un, re, able,* and *ment* are important for:

    a. Reading comprehension
    b. Word recognition
    c. Vocabulary building
    d. Reading fluency

92. VC, CVC, CCVC, CVCC, and CCVCC are among the types of:

    a. Homophones
    b. Closed syllables
    c. Monosyllabic words
    d. Polyglotal indicators

93. A student is taking a reading test. The teacher has blocked out a number of words. Each blank is assigned a set of three possible words. The student must select the correct word from each set so that the text makes sense. The student is taking:

    a. A cloze test
    b. A maze test
    c. A multiple-choice quiz
    d. A vocabulary test

94. When working with English Language Learners, the teacher should:

    a. Avoid idioms and slang, involve students in hands-on activities, reference students' prior knowledge, and speak slowly
    b. Speak slowly, use monosyllabic words whenever possible, repeat each sentence three times before moving to the next sentence, and employ idioms but not slang
    c. Use monosyllabic words whenever possible, repeat key instructions three times but not in a row, reference students' prior knowledge, and have students keep a journal of new vocabulary
    d. Have students keep a journal of new vocabulary, reference students' prior knowledge, speak slowly, and involve students in hands-on activities

95. Editing involves:

    a. Correcting surface features such as sentence fragments, spelling, and punctuation
    b. Fine-tuning the underlying structure of the piece to make the theme stand out
    c. Reconsidering ideas, adding or subtracting information, and changing the underlying structure
    d. Adding illustrations, charts, and other useful addenda

96. A seventh grader has never had much success with reading. Her ability to decode is rudimentary; she stops and starts when reading, frequently loses her place, or misreads an important word. She doesn't seem aware of where errors occur, or she does not attempt to correct them. When asked to tell about what she's read, her comprehension is minimal, to help her, instructional focus on which of the following would be most useful?

    a. Carefully organized lessons in decoding, sight words, vocabulary, and comprehension at least three to five times a week. These mini-lessons must be extremely clear, with the parts broken down to the lowest common denominator. The more tightly interwoven and systematized the instruction, the better chance this student will have

    b. A weekly lesson focusing on one aspect of reading. This student will be overwhelmed if too many strategies are offered at once. The instruction should focus first on recognizing sight words, then letter–sound association. Next, the girl needs an understanding of the rules of syntax.

    c. The student isn't trying. Her instruction should be aimed at helping her learn to be self-motivated and disciplined in her approach to learning

    d. Comprehension strategies will help her grasp the overall meaning of a text. From there she can begin to drill down until she's able to combine various approaches that, working together, will enable her to read

97. Silent reading fluency can best be assessed by:

    a. Having the student retell or summarize the material to determine how much was understood

    b. Giving a written test that covers plot, theme, character development, sequence of events, rising action, climax, falling action, and outcome. A student must test at a 95% accuracy rate to be considered fluent at silent reading

    c. Giving a three-minute Test of Silent Contextual Reading Fluency four times a year. The student is presented with text in which spaces between words and all punctuation have been removed. The student must divide one word from another with slash marks, as in the following example: The/little/sailboat/bobbed/so/far/in/the/distance/it/looked/like/a/toy. The more words a student accurately separates, the higher her silent reading fluency score

    d. Silent reading fluency cannot be assessed. It is a private act between the reader and the text and does not invite critique

98. A high school teacher has given her students an assignment to write a non-rhyming poem of three lines. The first and last lines each contain five syllables, and the middle line contains seven syllables. The students are writing a:

    a. Limerick
    b. Metaphor
    c. Villanelle
    d. Haiku

99. "Verbal dyspraxia" refers to:

    a. Trouble with the physical act of writing
    b. Confusing word or sentence order while speaking
    c. Misplacement of letters within words
    d. An inability to process verbal information

100. "Coarticulation" affects:
   a. Blending awareness
   b. Phonemic awareness
   c. Sequencing
   d. Aural awareness

Answers and Explanations

1. A: Homophones. Homophones are a type of homonym that sound alike, but are spelled differently and have different meanings. Other examples are *two, to,* and *too; their, they're,* and *there.*

2. C: Argumentative essay. The goal of a persuasive essay is to convince the reader that the author's position or opinion on a controversial topic is correct. That opinion or position is called the argument. A persuasive essay argues a series of points, supported by facts and evidence.

3. D: Rate, accuracy, and prosody. Fluent readers are able to read smoothly and comfortably at a steady pace (rate). The more quickly a child reads, the greater the chance of leaving out a word or substituting one word for another (for example, *sink* instead of *shrink*). Fluent readers are able to maintain accuracy without sacrificing rate. Fluent readers also stress important words in a text, group words into rhythmic phrases, and read with intonation (prosody).

4. B: The number of unrecognizable words an English Language Learner encounters when reading a passage or listening to a teacher. Language load is one of the barriers English Language Learners face. To lighten this load, a teacher can rephrase, eliminate unnecessary words, divide complex sentences into smaller units, and teach essential vocabulary before the student begins the lesson.

5. A: A vowel. A syllable is a minimal sound unit arranged around a vowel. For example, *academic* has four syllables: *a/ca/dem/ic.* It is possible for a syllable to be a single vowel, as in the above example. It is not possible for a syllable to be a single consonant.

6. C: Fail, producing students at a Frustration reading level. Those reading below grade level are likely to give up entirely. Those reading at grade level are likely to get frustrated and form habits that will actually slow down their development. Giving students texts that are too far beyond their reach produces frustrated readers. In an effort to succeed, frustrated writers are likely to apply strategies that have worked for them in the past but cannot work in this case because the text is simply beyond them. Looking for contextual clues to understand the meaning of unfamiliar words requires that most of the words in the passage are familiar. Breaking unfamiliar words into individual phonemes or syllables can be effective, but not if the number of such words is excessive. In this case, students below reading level and students at reading level will become frustrated when the skills that have worked for them in the past now fail.

7. C: Tier-two words. Tier-two words are words that are used with high frequency across a variety of disciplines or words with multiple meanings. They are characteristic of mature language users. Knowing these words is crucial to attaining an acceptable level of reading comprehension and communication skills.

8. C: Reading at her Independent reading level. When reading independently, students are at the correct level if they read with at least 97% accuracy.

9. B: To correct an error in reading a student has made, specifically clarifying where and how the error was made so that the student can avoid similar errors in the future. A reading teacher offers corrective feedback to a student in order to explain why a particular error in reading is, in fact, an error. Corrective feedback is specific; it locates where and how the student went astray so that similar errors can be avoided in future reading.

- 127 -

10. C: Content-specific words. Because these words are specific to paleontology, it's unlikely the students know their meanings. Without understanding what these words mean, the students would not be able to understand the content of the passage they were about to read.

11. B: Prior knowledge is knowledge the student brings from previous life or learning experiences to the act of reading. It is not possible for a student to fully comprehend new knowledge without first integrating it with prior knowledge. Prior knowledge, which rises from experience and previous learning, provides a framework by which new knowledge gained from the act of reading can be integrated. Every act of reading enriches a student's well of prior knowledge and increases that student's future ability to comprehend more fully any new knowledge acquired through reading.

12. B: Understanding of context and vocabulary. In a cloze test, a reader is given a text with certain words blocked out. The reader must be able to determine probable missing words based on contextual clues. In order to supply these words, the reader must already know them.

13. A: Common words with irregular spelling. Sight words occur in many types of writing; they are high-frequency words. Sight words are also words with irregular spelling. Some examples of sight words include *talk, some,* and *the.* Fluent readers need to recognize these words visually.

14. D: Consonant digraph. A consonant digraph is group of consonants in which all letters represent a single sound.

15. A: Phonological awareness. Phonemic awareness is the ability to recognize sounds within words. Segmenting words and blending sounds are components of phonemic awareness. Phonological awareness includes an understanding of multiple components of spoken language. Ability to hear individual words within a vocalized stream and ability to identify spoken syllables are types of phonological awareness.

16. A: Letter–sound correspondence. Letter–sound correspondence relies on the relationship between a spoken sound or group of sounds and the letters conventionally used in English to write them.

17. A: Strategy instruction. Strategic instruction involves teaching a methodic approach to solving a reading problem. It consists of strategies done in steps which aid the reader in eliminating incorrect responses.

18. D: Familiar, frequently used words that do not need to be taught beyond primary grades. Common or basic words are the first tier of three-tier words. These words are widely used across the spoken and written spectrum. Some examples are *walk, go, wish, the, look, happy,* and *always.* This essential vocabulary is taught early in a reader's instruction, and beyond that it need not be taught.

19. B: The number of phonemes. A phoneme is the smallest measure of language sound. English language phonemes, about 40 in number, are composed of individual letters as well as letter combinations. A number of letters have more than one associated sound. For example, "c" can be pronounced as a hard "c" (cake) or a soft "c" (Cynthia). Vowels in particular have a number of possible pronunciations.

20. B: Consonant blend. Consonant blend refers to a group of consonants in which each letter represents a separate sound.

21. A: Fewer than 100 words in the time given. At the beginning of the school year, second-grade students should be able to read 50–80 words per minute. By the time they are well into the school year, second-grade-level reading is tracked at 85 words per minute.

22. D: None; sight words cannot be decoded. Readers must learn to recognize these words as wholes on sight. Sight words have irregular spelling. Segmenting them into syllables or using a phonemic approach are ineffective strategies to aid a reader in recognizing a sight word, because these approaches depend on rules a sight word doesn't follow. Word families group words that share common patterns of consonants and vowels. The spelling of those words is therefore regular, because they follow a predictable pattern. Sight words are irregular and do not follow a predictable pattern and must be instantaneously recognized for writing fluency. No decoding is useful.

23. D: It is impossible to include every text desired into the language curriculum—there are simply too many good books, stories, poems, speeches, and media available. Teachers must first think about what skills their students need to acquire, as well as what skills they have already mastered. In designing activities for class, a good teacher will start first with the purpose for instruction (or perceiving oral or visual text such as video or music). For example, purposes of reading can include: reading for information; reading for enjoyment; understanding a message; identifying main or supporting ideas; or developing an appreciation for artistic expression/perception. Once the purpose or intended learning outcome has been identified, the teacher will have a much better idea of which texts, strategies, and activities will support that purpose.

24. C: Alphabetic principle. The act of decoding involves first recognizing the sounds individual letters and letter groups make, and then blending the sounds to read the word. A child decoding the word *spin*, for example, would first pronounce *sp/i/n* as individual sound units. She then would repeat the sounds, smoothly blending them. Because decoding involves understanding letters and their sounds, it is sometimes known as the alphabetic principle.

25. C: Students can easily become bored or disinterested in reading if they are not exposed to a variety of reading texts. Also, reading can be overwhelming or frustrating for students who are still learning to read fluently or to comprehend what they read. By incorporating media, oral stories, and various types of print, students of all ability levels can build both fluency and comprehension skills. This approach also enables the teacher and students to discuss the relationship between all aspects of literacy, including speaking, listening, thinking, viewing, and reading.

26. A: Oral. Phonological awareness refers to an understanding of the sounds a word makes. While phonological awareness leads to fluent reading skills, activities designed to develop an awareness of word sounds are, by definition, oral.

27. B: Vocabulary. Strategizing in order to understand the meaning of a word, knowing multiple meanings of a single word, and applying background knowledge to glean a word's meaning are all ways in which an effective reader enhances vocabulary. Other skills include an awareness of word parts and word origins, the ability to apply word meanings in a variety of content areas, and a delight in learning the meanings of unfamiliar words.

28. C: She is reading at an Instructional level. In one minute, a student who misreads one or less than one word per twenty words, or with 95%–100% accuracy, is at an Independent reading level. A student who misreads one or less than one word per ten words, or with 90%–95% accuracy, is at an Instructional level. A student misreading more than one word out of ten, or with less than 90% accuracy, is at a Frustration level.

29. D: Decoding depends on an understanding of letter–sound relationships. As soon as a child understands enough letters and their correspondent sounds to read a few words, decoding should be introduced. The act of decoding involves first recognizing the sounds individual letters and letter groups in a word make and then blending the sounds to read the word. It's important to introduce the strategy as soon as a child knows enough letters and their corresponding sounds to read simple words.

30. C: Cause–effect words. Signal words give the reader hints about the purpose of a particular passage. Some signal words are concerned with comparing/contrasting, some with cause and effect, some with temporal sequencing, some with physical location, and some with a problem and its solution. The words *since, whether,* and *accordingly* are words used when describing an outcome. Outcomes have causes.

31. A: Outcome. Story action can be analyzed in terms of rising action, story climax, falling action, and resolution. Rising action consists of those events that occur before and lead up to the story's most dramatic moment, or climax. The climax occurs toward the end of the book, but rarely, if ever, right at the end. Following the climax, the consequences of that dramatic moment are termed falling action. The story reaches resolution with the outcome of the falling action.

32. C: Locate the vowels, then locate familiar word parts. Syllables are organized around vowels. In order to determine the syllables, this student should begin by locating the vowels. It's possible to have a syllable that is a single vowel (*a/gain*). It isn't possible to have a syllable that is a single consonant. Once the word has been broken into its component syllables the reader is able to study the syllables to find ones that are familiar and might give her a clue as to the word's meaning, such as certain prefixes or suffixes.

33. A: Nothing. These children are simply at an early stage in the reading/writing process. When emergent readers become aware of the connections between letters and sounds, and between reading and writing, they want to practice the skills they see proficient readers use. While a proficient writer knows that letters are grouped into words and that words are constructed into sentences that move from left to right and from the top of the page to the bottom, an emergent reader/writer knows only that letters magically contain sounds that other people can read. It is necessary for children to pass through early stages in which they scribble-write and pretend they are scripting letters, which leads to a stage in which they actually do write the initial letter of a word all over the page. Next, the emergent reader/writer will write the initial letter of many of the words that belong in the sentence and will write them sequentially. KJM, for example, might mean *the cat chased a mouse.*

34. A: Scripting the end-sound to a word (KT=cat); leaving space between words; writing from the top left to the top right of the page, and from top to bottom. Each of these steps is progressively more abstract. Scripting the end-sound to a word helps a young writer recognize that words have beginnings and endings. This naturally leads to the willingness to separate words with white space so that they stand as individual entities. Once this step is reached, the child realizes that in English, writing progresses from left to right and from the top of the page to the bottom.

35. B: Ask the students to read their stories to her. Suggest they visit other children in the class and read to each of them. The teacher should encourage these students by "reading" what they have written, even if what she reads is incorrect. She might misread KJM as *Kathy jumped rope with Mandy.* Most children will not be upset by this, but will correct the teacher's misreading by reading what the letters really mean.

36. D: The teacher should encourage all students to "read" picture books from the first day of school. Talking about the pictures from page to page gives young readers the idea that books are arranged sequentially. Pictures also offer narrative coherence and contextual clues. Emergent readers who are encouraged to enjoy books will more readily embrace the act of reading. Holding a book and turning pages gives young readers a familiarity with them.

37. A: Most adults can understand the relationship between oral and written language: components of oral language have representational symbols that can be written and decoded. However, most normally-developing children acquire spoken language first and begin to develop reading and writing skills as they approach school-age. Many children are first exposed to the concept of written language when an adult introduces books or other written texts. However, a child's ability to read and write develops over time and is dependent on the development of physiological processes such as hearing, sight, and fine motor skills for writing. Written language development also typically requires direct instruction. Most children must be taught to read and write and rarely learn these skills simply by observing others.

38. C: Identify and use groups of letters that occur in a word family. Analogizing is based on recognizing the pattern of letters in words that share sound similarities. If the pattern is found at the end of a family of words, it is called a *rhyme*. Some examples of rhyme are *rent, sent, bent,* and *dent.* If the pattern is found at the beginning of the family of words, it is frequently a consonant *blend* such as *street, stripe,* or *strong,* in which all the letters are pronounced, or the pattern is a consonant digraph, in which the letters are taken together to represent a single sound such as in *phone, phonics,* or *phantom.*

39. A: Useful. The child will feel more confident because the story is already familiar. She will also feel that the lesson is a conversation of sorts, and that she is communicating successfully. She will be motivated to learn the English words because they are meaningful and highly charged. As a newly arrived immigrant, the child feels overwhelmed. Presenting her with a book of folk tales from her country tells her that she needn't lose her culture in order to function in this one. It also comforts her by reminding her that her past and present are linked. Allowing her to speak in Korean helps her express herself without fear of judgment or failure. Presenting her with an English vocabulary that is meaningful ensures that she will eagerly embrace these words, her first words in her new language.

40. D: Cultural load. Cultural load is concerned with how the relationship between language and culture can help or hinder learning. By using the Korean folk tale, the teacher offered the child the opportunity to learn new words in a context that was culturally familiar. By demonstrating respect for her student's culture, she helped lighten the cultural load.

41. C: Right and left; left. Researchers have discovered through brain imaging that a dyslexic reader uses both sides of the brain. Non-dyslexic readers use only the left side.

42. B: Revising. Revision (literally, re+vision) is the act of "seeing again." When revising, writers examine what they have written in order to improve the meaning of the work. Fine-tuning word choices, moving information to another location, and adding or deleting words are all acts of revision.

43. D: Prefixes, appearing at the beginning of base words to change their meanings. Suffixes appear at the end of words. Prefixes are attached to the beginning of words to change their meanings. *Un+happy, bi+monthly,* and *re+examine* are prefixes that, by definition, change the meanings of the words to which they are attached.

44. D: Dog, sit, leg. CVC words are composed of a consonant, a vowel, and a consonant. To learn to read them, students must be familiar with the letters used and their sounds. A teacher can present a word like *sit* to students who also know the consonants *b/f/h/p* and ask them to create a word family of other CVC words. The students will be able to read *bit, fit, hit,* and *pit* because they are similar to the word *sit* they have just learned.

45. C: Context. By considering the other words in the story, the student can determine the missing words. The student is depending on the information supplied by the rest of the story. This information puts the story into context.

46. D: All of the above. Metacognition means a reader's awareness of her own reading processes as she improves reading comprehension. Other elements of metacognition include awareness of areas in the text where the reader fails to comprehend and an understanding of how the text is structured.

47. A: Cooperative learning and reading comprehension. Cooperative learning occurs when a group of students at various levels of reading ability have goals in common. Reading comprehension is achieved through reading both orally and silently, developing vocabulary, a reader's ability to predict what will occur in a piece of writing, a reader's ability to summarize the main points in a piece of writing, and a reader's ability to reflect on the text's meaning and connect that meaning to another text or personal experience.

48. B: Understanding the meaning of words that are not familiar. Context cues offer insight into the probable meaning of unfamiliar words.

49. C: Observe the child over the course of a week or two. Draw her into conversation and determine if her vocabulary is limited, if she displays emotional problems, or if her reticence could have another cause. Note how the child interacts with others in the class. Does she ever initiate conversation? If another child initiates, does she respond? Until the teacher monitors the child's verbal abilities and habits, she cannot determine if the lack of interaction suggests a learning disability, an emotional problem, or simply a shy personality. The teacher should informally observe the child over a period of time, noting if and when she initiates or responds to oral language, if she is reading with apparent comprehension, if her vocabulary is limited, and the degree to which the child is interested in understanding.

50. C: There are many genres from which students can choose to read. The most elemental distinction between genres consists of fiction and non-fiction, the latter referring to stories or texts that are true, or factual. Fictional texts can fall into a variety of categories. Realistic fiction seems as though it could be true. These stories involve realistic characters and settings with which readers can often identify. This type of fiction can treat different subjects, but it still must be relatable in nature.

51. C: Persuasive. The author is hoping to persuade or convince young readers to avoid sex by providing them with facts as well as by using rhetorical devices such as dispelling opposing arguments.

52. C: They meet to discuss areas the teacher is most concerned about and decide on the teacher's goals. In order to best achieve goals, those goals must be understood and established.

53. D: Being able to identify rhyme is an important element of phonological awareness. Young children use language in a solely oral way. Oral language is composed of separate sounds that are represented in written form by the alphabet. In order to read, a child must first have a sense of the

sounds that are used in English (phonological awareness). By helping children hear the difference between rhyming and non-rhyming words, the teacher is preparing them to make the transition to sound–letter association and word families.

54. A: Closed, open, silent *e*, vowel team, vowel-*r*, and consonant-*le*. A closed syllable ends with a consonant, such as *cat*. Open syllables end with a vowel, such as *he*. Vowel team syllables contain two vowels working together, such as *main*. Vowel-*r* syllables such as *er* and *or* frequently occur as suffixes. Consonant-*le* syllables also typically occur as suffixes, such as *battle* or *terrible*.

55. A: Strategies to increase comprehension and to build vocabulary. The student should receive instruction focused on just those areas in which he is exhibiting difficulty. Improved vocabulary will give him greater skill at comprehending the meaning of a particular text. Strategies focused on enhancing comprehension together with a stronger vocabulary will provide the greatest help.

56. B: Through a combination of standardized testing, informal teacher observations, attention to grades, objective-linked assessments, and systematized charting of data over time. Reading comprehension and vocabulary cannot be sufficiently assessed with occasional, brief studies. Continuous observation, high-stakes and standardized testing, attention to grades, and closely tracking the outcomes of objective-linked assessments are interrelated tools that, when systematically organized, offer a thorough understanding of students' strengths and weaknesses.

57. A: An Oral Reading Fluency assessment. ORF stands for oral reading fluency. This assessment measures the words correct per minute (WCPM) by subtracting the number of errors made from the total number of words orally read in a one- to two-minute period of time. It is used to find a student's Instructional reading level, to identify readers who are having difficulties, and to track developing fluency and word recognition over time.

58. D: Round-robin reading is a common practice in language arts classes and has been for many years. In this process, students take turns reading aloud for their peers. Other students are asked to follow along silently in their texts while a peer is reading. This strategy does provide a way for students to read texts in class and include as many students as possible, which is often the intended outcome. However, this process often creates a boring atmosphere, since only one student at a time is actively engaged. While that student is reading, other students may become distracted by their own thoughts, other school work, or off-task interaction with each other; all of these issues subvert the intended outcome of the process. There is rarely enough time for each student to practice reading aloud to build students' reading fluency or comprehension in significant ways.

59. D: Especially important to English Language Learners and students with reading disabilities. Word recognition is required for reading fluency and is important to all readers, but it is especially so to English Language Learners and students with reading disabilities. It can be effectively taught through precisely calibrated word study instruction designed to provide readers with reading and writing strategies for successful word analysis.

60. A: Proficiency with oral language enhances students' phonemic awareness and increases vocabulary. Understanding that words are scripted with specific letters representing specific sounds is essential to decoding a text. Students cannot effectively learn to read without the ability to decode. An enhanced vocabulary supports the act of reading; the larger an emergent reader's vocabulary, the more quickly he will learn to read. He will be able to decode more words, which he can organize into word families, which he can use to decode unfamiliar words.

61. C: Read the documents quickly, looking for key words in order to gather the basic premise of each. Skimming allows a reader to quickly gain a broad understanding of a piece of writing in order

- 133 -

to determine if a more thorough reading is warranted. Skimming allows students who are researching a topic on the Internet or in print to consider a substantial body of information in order to select only that of particular relevance.

62. B: Expository. Expository essays clarify an idea, explain an event, or interpret facts. The position the author takes is often supported with statistics, quotations, or other evidence researched from a variety of sources.

63. B: Persuasive. A persuasive essay takes a strong position about a controversial topic and offers factual evidence to support this position. The goal of a persuasive paper is to convince the audience that the claim is true based on the evidence provided.

64. A: However, the myth of "safe cigarettes," questions about nicotine addiction, and denials about the dangers of secondhand smoke have proven to be propaganda and lies. A thesis statement offers a hypothesis or opinion that the remainder of the paper then sets out to prove. Oftentimes, the thesis statement also offers a clear road map of the paper, foreshadowing the focuses of the paragraphs that follow and the order in which they will appear.

65. D: The myth of "safe cigarettes," questions about nicotine addiction, and the dangers of secondhand smoke. These three foci are presented in the thesis statement in this order and will be fleshed out in the following three paragraphs as the body of the essay.

66. C: Example. Example essays, also called illustration essays, are simple, straightforward pieces that depend on clearly described examples to make their points. An example essay isn't trying to convince the reader (argumentative), compare similar or dissimilar things (compare/contrast), or point to relationships such as cause and effect. Often, example essays teach the reader how to accomplish something or about something.

67. C: Are homophones. Homophones are words that are pronounced the same, but differ in meaning. For example, a bride wears a 2 caret ring, but a horse eats a carrot.

68. A: Collaborative learning. A group of students working together on a project are applying numerous learning strategies at once. Collaborative learning is a hands-on approach that actively involves students in the learning process. Students involved in collaborative learning typically retain the lesson better.

69. C: Biography. A biography relates information about part of the life of an individual. An autobiography is a biography about the writer's own life. A memoir is also autobiographical, but focuses on a theme. Historical fiction uses a setting or event based in historical fact as the background for characters and/or action that is invented.

70. C: Students will do online research about the cultural, economic, or political events that were occurring during the specific time about which they've written. By researching the historic setting that cradled the events their interviewee discussed, students are simultaneously broadening their understanding of the context and working in a different content area.

71. B: Brainstorming and a compare/contrast strategy. Brainstorming is a prewriting activity in which an individual or group responds to a specific question by considering any and all responses that arise without editing, prioritizing, or selecting. Once the brainstorming session is complete, students look at the results and eliminate any responses that are not useful, then group and prioritize the remaining responses. In this example, the students are having a collaborative learning experience in that they are brainstorming together; however, collaborative learning is not a

- 134 -

strategy per se, but is the outcome of a strategy. The students are also employing a compare/contrast strategy in that they are looking both at how the two writing styles share common elements and how they are distinct.

72. C: Writing styles. Both Anderson and the Grimms wrote in the same genre, that of fairy tales. Genre refers to types of writing. Mystery, romance, adventure, historical fiction, and fairy tales are some examples of genres. A genre can include many different authors and writing styles. These students are being asked to compare two distinct writing styles within a single genre in order to locate similarities and differences.

73. B: Comprehension. This exercise requires students to examine the authors' use of setting, plot, pacing, word choice, syntactical structures, narration, mood, metaphors, point of view, voice, and character development to find ways in which they are similar as well as different. In so doing, the students are discovering that language shapes meaning in ways both subtle and profound.

74. C: The importance of culture to meaning. Authors make thousands of decisions in the act of writing. What point of view to take, how much weight to give an event, what to reveal about a character, and what words will most effectively express the writer's intention are but a few of these decisions. While many of these decisions are consciously artistic choices, many are unconscious and imbedded in the cultural expectations of time and place in which the author has lived. To understand a text to the fullest degree possible, it is necessary to read it with an eye to the cultural framework from whence it came.

75. A: Give each child a piece of drawing paper that has been folded in half and then again, creating four boxes, along with a piece that has not been folded. The teacher should then ask the students to draw a cartoon about the story. Each of the first four boxes will show the events in order. The second page is to show how the story ends. When a child is able to visually see the way a familiar story has unfolded, that child can find causal or thematic connections in the action that increases her comprehension of the story overall. Asking the class to draw a single picture or to draw the beginning and end doesn't sufficiently demonstrate the importance of order to meaning. While some first graders may be able to create their own cartoon stories that demonstrate a logical series of events, many first graders are not yet ready to organize thought into a linear progression.

76. A: Sonnet. There are three primary types of sonnets. The Shakespearean sonnet is specifically what these students are reading. A Spenserian sonnet is also composed of three four-line stanzas followed by a two-line couplet; however, the rhymes are not contained within each stanza but spill from one stanza to the next (*abab bcbc cdcd ee*). A Petrarchan sonnet divides into an eight-line stanza and a six-line stanza.

77. D: Compare and contrast. Asking children to write a list provides them with a visual model that is a side-by-side comparison of the two countries. In creating that visual model, each student first has to organize his or her thoughts mentally, deciding whether each particular item under consideration shares more or less in common with the other.

78. D: Teachers will observe a variety of developmental arcs when teaching reading, since all students learn differently. It is very important to understand which instances are normal in the course of learning and which signal a learning difficulty. Barrett is still exhibiting confusion over certain letter-sounds, typically when the letters look similar. At his age, this difficulty could suggest that Barrett has an issue with reading that could be addressed by a reading specialist. The other three choices describe normal behaviors that are commonly exhibited by children when they are learning to read. Choice C, Noelle, may describe an instance in which a student is having a learning

problem. However, the teacher will need more information about Noelle's reading skills besides her reluctance to read before making a determination about how to proceed.

79. A: The words in this question prompt are most often used to refer to *sounds* made while reading. Initial/onset, medial, and final sounds are decoded in the beginning, middle, and end of words. When a teacher needs to assess an emergent or struggling reader's ability to differentiate between sounds in words, he or she may use a phonological awareness assessment. This tool will provide the teacher with information about the student's current ability to decode or encode words.

80. A: Dysgraphia. Dysgraphic individuals have difficulty with the physical act of writing. They find holding and manipulating a pencil problematic. Their letters are primitively formed, and their handwriting is illegible.

81. B: Cliché. While "Pretty as a picture" is a simile (comparison of two unlike things using *like* or *as*), its overuse has turned it into a cliché. A cliché is a trite platitude.

82. B: Vocabulary. The tightly controlled syllabic requirements will cause students to search for words outside their normal vocabularies that will fit the rigid framework and still express the writer's intended meanings. Often, students will rediscover a word whose meaning they know, but they don't often use.

83. C: Brainstorming a list of verbs that mean ways of talking or ways of going, then adding them to the word wall along with some nouns that specify common topics. Second graders aren't developmentally ready for a thesaurus; most will believe that any words in a particular list are interchangeable. For example, a student who wrote *my little sister walks like a baby* might find the verbs *strut, sidle,* and *amble* in the thesaurus. None of these verbs would be an appropriate substitution. Supplementing a noun with an adjective often results in flat writing: *There's a tree in my yard* might become *There's a nice tree in my big yard.* Adjectives such as *pretty, fun, cute, funny,* and so forth don't add much in terms of meaning, but they are the adjectives younger writers reach for first. A more specific noun is both more meaningful and more interesting. *There's a weeping willow in my yard* is evocative.

84. B: Scaffolding refers to any kind of special instruction designed to help students learn a new or challenging concept. There are countless forms of scaffolding techniques. The three techniques mentioned in the question prompt are all used to facilitate student understanding of a given text or a concept taught within the text. Scaffolding should not be confused with modeling strategies, which refer to the process of demonstrating how something should be done before a student tries it on his or her own.

85. C: *Drip, chirp, splash, giggle.* Onomatopoeia refers to words that sound like what they represent.

86. D: It offers a systematic approach to untangling the wide variety of vowel sounds when an unfamiliar word is encountered. Code knowledge, also called orthographic tendencies, is a helpful approach to decoding a word when multiple pronunciation possibilities exist. Example in the words *toe, go, though,* and *low,* the long O sound is written in a variety of ways. A code knowledge approach teaches a reader to first try a short vowel sound. If that doesn't help, the reader should consider the different ways the vowel or vowel groups can be pronounced, based on what he knows about other words.

87. D: Assess and target areas needing improvement as well as areas of greatest strength for each student to ensure that all members of a class are receiving instruction tailored to their specific needs.

88. A: Clarifying the goal, modeling strategies, and offering explanations geared to a student's level of understanding. Explicit instruction is well organized and structured, and it offers easily understood steps and depends in part on frequent reference to previously learned materials.

89. B: Scaffolding. Using this strategic approach, a teacher assigns a task that is just beyond the student's current level. The teacher encourages the student's attempts at comprehension by offering various supports that largely depend on prior knowledge, in order to develop the student's willingness to move forward into uncharted territory as a confident independent learner.

90. D: There are various cueing systems that readers can use to help them understand how to read or comprehend unfamiliar words. Semantic cueing helps with understanding word meaning; the reader uses the meaning of the words around an unfamiliar word to understand what that word means. Syntactical cueing can also be called "grammatical cueing," in which a reader uses the syntax of a sentence to understand more about an unfamiliar word. Graphophonic cueing is most useful in decoding, or breaking words down into smaller components new words.

91. A: Reading comprehension. Prefixes and suffixes change the meanings of the root word to which they are attached. A student who understands that *un* means "not" will be able to decipher the meanings of words such as *unwanted, unhappy,* or *unreasonable.*

92. B: Closed syllables. Closed syllables are those that end with a consonant. *At, dog, spit, duck,* and *pluck* are all examples of closed syllables.

93. B: A maze test. A maze test is a specific type of cloze test. In a cloze test, words are deleted and the reader must supply the missing words using contextual clues and vocabulary that is familiar. A maze test is a multiple-choice application of a cloze test.

94. A: Avoid idioms and slang, involve students in hands-on activities, reference students' prior knowledge, and speak slowly. Teachers of English Language Learners should not employ idioms and slang in their instruction because these informal uses of speech are likely to confuse the students. Involving students in hands-on activities such as group reading and language play makes the experience both more meaningful and more immediate. New knowledge can only be absorbed by attaching it to prior knowledge, referencing what students already know is essential. Speaking slowly to English Language Learners is important, because they are processing what is being said at a slower rate than a native speaker.

95. A: Correcting surface features such as sentence fragments, spelling, and punctuation. Editing is the final step in the writing process. The writer has already decided the ideas or events are in proper order, have been sufficiently described, and are clear. Now the writer turns her attention to surface features, "scrubbing" errors in spelling, punctuation, and syntax from the writing.

96. A: Carefully organized lessons in decoding, sight words, vocabulary, and comprehension at least three to five times a week. These mini-lessons must be extremely clear, with the parts broken down to the lowest common denominator. The more tightly interwoven and systematized the instruction, the better chance this student will have. This type of learner needs, first and foremost, instruction that has been highly organized into a system that will make sense to her. If possible, she should receive private instruction on a daily basis. The instruction needs to focus on decoding, recognizing words, reading with increasing fluency, enhancing vocabulary, and comprehension. She should be working at the Instructional level, or with texts she can read with at least 90% accuracy.

97. C: Giving a three-minute Test of Silent Contextual Reading Fluency four times a year. The student is presented with text in which spaces between words and all punctuation have been

- 137 -

removed. The student must divide one word from another with slash marks, as in the following example: *The/little/sailboat/bobbed/so/far/in/the/distance/it/looked/like/a/toy*. The more words a student accurately separates, then the higher her silent reading fluency score. Silent reading fluency can be monitored over time by giving the Test of Silent Contextual Reading Fluency (TSCRF) four times a year. A similar assessment tool is the Test of Silent Word Reading Fluency (TOSWRF), in which words of increasing complexity are given as a single, undifferentiated, and unpunctuated strand. As with the TSCRF, three minutes are given for the student to separate each word from the next. *Itwillcannotschoolbecomeagendaconsistentphilosophysuperfluous* is an example of such a strand.

98. D: Haiku. Based on a Japanese form of poetry, haiku have become popular with students and teachers alike. Reading and writing haiku helps younger students become aware of syllables and helps older students learn about subtleties of vocabulary.

99. B: Confusing word or sentence order while speaking. Dyspraxic individuals do not process spoken language sequentially due to a neurological distortion. The dislocation of sounds within a word, such as vocalizing *lamp* instead of *palm*, is one indication of verbal dyspraxia.

100. B: Phonemic awareness. Vocalizing words involves arranging a series of continuous, voice, unvoiced, and stop sounds. As one sound is being uttered, the tongue and lips are already assuming the shape required by the next sound in the word. This process, which is not conscious, can distort individual sounds. One sound can slur into another, clip the end of the previous sound, or flatten or heighten a sound. For children who have difficulty hearing distinct phonemic sounds, individual instruction may be required.

How to Overcome Test Anxiety

Just the thought of taking a test is enough to make most people a little nervous. A test is an important event that can have a long-term impact on your future, so it's important to take it seriously and it's natural to feel anxious about performing well. But just because anxiety is normal, that doesn't mean that it's helpful in test taking, or that you should simply accept it as part of your life. Anxiety can have a variety of effects. These effects can be mild, like making you feel slightly nervous, or severe, like blocking your ability to focus or remember even a simple detail.

If you experience test anxiety—whether severe or mild—it's important to know how to beat it. To discover this, first you need to understand what causes test anxiety.

Causes of Test Anxiety

While we often think of anxiety as an uncontrollable emotional state, it can actually be caused by simple, practical things. One of the most common causes of test anxiety is that a person does not feel adequately prepared for their test. This feeling can be the result of many different issues such as poor study habits or lack of organization, but the most common culprit is time management. Starting to study too late, failing to organize your study time to cover all of the material, or being distracted while you study will mean that you're not well prepared for the test. This may lead to cramming the night before, which will cause you to be physically and mentally exhausted for the test. Poor time management also contributes to feelings of stress, fear, and hopelessness as you realize you are not well prepared but don't know what to do about it.

Other times, test anxiety is not related to your preparation for the test but comes from unresolved fear. This may be a past failure on a test, or poor performance on tests in general. It may come from comparing yourself to others who seem to be performing better or from the stress of living up to expectations. Anxiety may be driven by fears of the future—how failure on this test would affect your educational and career goals. These fears are often completely irrational, but they can still negatively impact your test performance.

> **Review Video: 3 Reasons You Have Test Anxiety**
> Visit mometrix.com/academy and enter code: 428468

Elements of Test Anxiety

As mentioned earlier, test anxiety is considered to be an emotional state, but it has physical and mental components as well. Sometimes you may not even realize that you are suffering from test anxiety until you notice the physical symptoms. These can include trembling hands, rapid heartbeat, sweating, nausea, and tense muscles. Extreme anxiety may lead to fainting or vomiting. Obviously, any of these symptoms can have a negative impact on testing. It is important to recognize them as soon as they begin to occur so that you can address the problem before it damages your performance.

> **Review Video: 3 Ways to Tell You Have Test Anxiety**
> Visit mometrix.com/academy and enter code: 927847

The mental components of test anxiety include trouble focusing and inability to remember learned information. During a test, your mind is on high alert, which can help you recall information and stay focused for an extended period of time. However, anxiety interferes with your mind's natural processes, causing you to blank out, even on the questions you know well. The strain of testing during anxiety makes it difficult to stay focused, especially on a test that may take several hours. Extreme anxiety can take a huge mental toll, making it difficult not only to recall test information but even to understand the test questions or pull your thoughts together.

> **Review Video: How Test Anxiety Affects Memory**
> Visit mometrix.com/academy and enter code: 609003

Effects of Test Anxiety

Test anxiety is like a disease—if left untreated, it will get progressively worse. Anxiety leads to poor performance, and this reinforces the feelings of fear and failure, which in turn lead to poor performances on subsequent tests. It can grow from a mild nervousness to a crippling condition. If allowed to progress, test anxiety can have a big impact on your schooling, and consequently on your future.

Test anxiety can spread to other parts of your life. Anxiety on tests can become anxiety in any stressful situation, and blanking on a test can turn into panicking in a job situation. But fortunately, you don't have to let anxiety rule your testing and determine your grades. There are a number of relatively simple steps you can take to move past anxiety and function normally on a test and in the rest of life.

> **Review Video: How Test Anxiety Impacts Your Grades**
> Visit mometrix.com/academy and enter code: 939819

Physical Steps for Beating Test Anxiety

While test anxiety is a serious problem, the good news is that it can be overcome. It doesn't have to control your ability to think and remember information. While it may take time, you can begin taking steps today to beat anxiety.

Just as your first hint that you may be struggling with anxiety comes from the physical symptoms, the first step to treating it is also physical. Rest is crucial for having a clear, strong mind. If you are tired, it is much easier to give in to anxiety. But if you establish good sleep habits, your body and mind will be ready to perform optimally, without the strain of exhaustion. Additionally, sleeping well helps you to retain information better, so you're more likely to recall the answers when you see the test questions.

Getting good sleep means more than going to bed on time. It's important to allow your brain time to relax. Take study breaks from time to time so it doesn't get overworked, and don't study right before bed. Take time to rest your mind before trying to rest your body, or you may find it difficult to fall asleep.

> **Review Video: The Importance of Sleep for Your Brain**
> Visit mometrix.com/academy and enter code: 319338

Along with sleep, other aspects of physical health are important in preparing for a test. Good nutrition is vital for good brain function. Sugary foods and drinks may give a burst of energy but this burst is followed by a crash, both physically and emotionally. Instead, fuel your body with protein and vitamin-rich foods.

Also, drink plenty of water. Dehydration can lead to headaches and exhaustion, especially if your brain is already under stress from the rigors of the test. Particularly if your test is a long one, drink water during the breaks. And if possible, take an energy-boosting snack to eat between sections.

> **Review Video: How Diet Can Affect your Mood**
> Visit mometrix.com/academy and enter code: 624317

Along with sleep and diet, a third important part of physical health is exercise. Maintaining a steady workout schedule is helpful, but even taking 5-minute study breaks to walk can help get your blood pumping faster and clear your head. Exercise also releases endorphins, which contribute to a positive feeling and can help combat test anxiety.

When you nurture your physical health, you are also contributing to your mental health. If your body is healthy, your mind is much more likely to be healthy as well. So take time to rest, nourish your body with healthy food and water, and get moving as much as possible. Taking these physical steps will make you stronger and more able to take the mental steps necessary to overcome test anxiety.

> **Review Video: How to Stay Healthy and Prevent Test Anxiety**
> Visit mometrix.com/academy and enter code: 877894

Mental Steps for Beating Test Anxiety

Working on the mental side of test anxiety can be more challenging, but as with the physical side, there are clear steps you can take to overcome it. As mentioned earlier, test anxiety often stems from lack of preparation, so the obvious solution is to prepare for the test. Effective studying may be the most important weapon you have for beating test anxiety, but you can and should employ several other mental tools to combat fear.

First, boost your confidence by reminding yourself of past success—tests or projects that you aced. If you're putting as much effort into preparing for this test as you did for those, there's no reason you should expect to fail here. Work hard to prepare; then trust your preparation.

Second, surround yourself with encouraging people. It can be helpful to find a study group, but be sure that the people you're around will encourage a positive attitude. If you spend time with others who are anxious or cynical, this will only contribute to your own anxiety. Look for others who are motivated to study hard from a desire to succeed, not from a fear of failure.

Third, reward yourself. A test is physically and mentally tiring, even without anxiety, and it can be helpful to have something to look forward to. Plan an activity following the test, regardless of the outcome, such as going to a movie or getting ice cream.

When you are taking the test, if you find yourself beginning to feel anxious, remind yourself that you know the material. Visualize successfully completing the test. Then take a few deep, relaxing breaths and return to it. Work through the questions carefully but with confidence, knowing that you are capable of succeeding.

Developing a healthy mental approach to test taking will also aid in other areas of life. Test anxiety affects more than just the actual test—it can be damaging to your mental health and even contribute to depression. It's important to beat test anxiety before it becomes a problem for more than testing.

> **Review Video: Test Anxiety and Depression**
> Visit mometrix.com/academy and enter code: 904704

Study Strategy

Being prepared for the test is necessary to combat anxiety, but what does being prepared look like? You may study for hours on end and still not feel prepared. What you need is a strategy for test prep. The next few pages outline our recommended steps to help you plan out and conquer the challenge of preparation.

Step 1: Scope Out the Test

Learn everything you can about the format (multiple choice, essay, etc.) and what will be on the test. Gather any study materials, course outlines, or sample exams that may be available. Not only will this help you to prepare, but knowing what to expect can help to alleviate test anxiety.

Step 2: Map Out the Material

Look through the textbook or study guide and make note of how many chapters or sections it has. Then divide these over the time you have. For example, if a book has 15 chapters and you have five days to study, you need to cover three chapters each day. Even better, if you have the time, leave an extra day at the end for overall review after you have gone through the material in depth.

If time is limited, you may need to prioritize the material. Look through it and make note of which sections you think you already have a good grasp on, and which need review. While you are studying, skim quickly through the familiar sections and take more time on the challenging parts. Write out your plan so you don't get lost as you go. Having a written plan also helps you feel more in control of the study, so anxiety is less likely to arise from feeling overwhelmed at the amount to cover. A sample plan may look like this:

- Day 1: Skim chapters 1–4, study chapter 5 (especially pages 31–33)
- Day 2: Study chapters 6–7, skim chapters 8–9
- Day 3: Skim chapter 10, study chapters 11–12 (especially pages 87–90)
- Day 4: Study chapters 13–15
- Day 5: Overall review (focus most on chapters 5, 6, and 12), take practice test

Step 3: Gather Your Tools

Decide what study method works best for you. Do you prefer to highlight in the book as you study and then go back over the highlighted portions? Or do you type out notes of the important information? Or is it helpful to make flashcards that you can carry with you? Assemble the pens, index cards, highlighters, post-it notes, and any other materials you may need so you won't be distracted by getting up to find things while you study.

If you're having a hard time retaining the information or organizing your notes, experiment with different methods. For example, try color-coding by subject with colored pens, highlighters, or post-it notes. If you learn better by hearing, try recording yourself reading your notes so you can listen while in the car, working out, or simply sitting at your desk. Ask a friend to quiz you from your flashcards, or try teaching someone the material to solidify it in your mind.

Step 4: Create Your Environment

It's important to avoid distractions while you study. This includes both the obvious distractions like visitors and the subtle distractions like an uncomfortable chair (or a too-comfortable couch that makes you want to fall asleep). Set up the best study environment possible: good lighting and a comfortable work area. If background music helps you focus, you may want to turn it on, but otherwise keep the room quiet. If you are using a computer to take notes, be sure you don't have any other windows open, especially applications like social media, games, or anything else that could distract you. Silence your phone and turn off notifications. Be sure to keep water close by so you stay hydrated while you study (but avoid unhealthy drinks and snacks).

Also, take into account the best time of day to study. Are you freshest first thing in the morning? Try to set aside some time then to work through the material. Is your mind clearer in the afternoon or evening? Schedule your study session then. Another method is to study at the same time of day that you will take the test, so that your brain gets used to working on the material at that time and will be ready to focus at test time.

Step 5: Study!

Once you have done all the study preparation, it's time to settle into the actual studying. Sit down, take a few moments to settle your mind so you can focus, and begin to follow your study plan. Don't give in to distractions or let yourself procrastinate. This is your time to prepare so you'll be ready to fearlessly approach the test. Make the most of the time and stay focused.

Of course, you don't want to burn out. If you study too long you may find that you're not retaining the information very well. Take regular study breaks. For example, taking five minutes out of every hour to walk briskly, breathing deeply and swinging your arms, can help your mind stay fresh.

As you get to the end of each chapter or section, it's a good idea to do a quick review. Remind yourself of what you learned and work on any difficult parts. When you feel that you've mastered the material, move on to the next part. At the end of your study session, briefly skim through your notes again.

But while review is helpful, cramming last minute is NOT. If at all possible, work ahead so that you won't need to fit all your study into the last day. Cramming overloads your brain with more information than it can process and retain, and your tired mind may struggle to recall even previously learned information when it is overwhelmed with last-minute study. Also, the urgent nature of cramming and the stress placed on your brain contribute to anxiety. You'll be more likely to go to the test feeling unprepared and having trouble thinking clearly.

So don't cram, and don't stay up late before the test, even just to review your notes at a leisurely pace. Your brain needs rest more than it needs to go over the information again. In fact, plan to finish your studies by noon or early afternoon the day before the test. Give your brain the rest of the day to relax or focus on other things, and get a good night's sleep. Then you will be fresh for the test and better able to recall what you've studied.

Step 6: Take a practice test

Many courses offer sample tests, either online or in the study materials. This is an excellent resource to check whether you have mastered the material, as well as to prepare for the test format and environment.

Check the test format ahead of time: the number of questions, the type (multiple choice, free response, etc.), and the time limit. Then create a plan for working through them. For example, if you have 30 minutes to take a 60-question test, your limit is 30 seconds per question. Spend less time on the questions you know well so that you can take more time on the difficult ones.

If you have time to take several practice tests, take the first one open book, with no time limit. Work through the questions at your own pace and make sure you fully understand them. Gradually work up to taking a test under test conditions: sit at a desk with all study materials put away and set a timer. Pace yourself to make sure you finish the test with time to spare and go back to check your answers if you have time.

After each test, check your answers. On the questions you missed, be sure you understand why you missed them. Did you misread the question (tests can use tricky wording)? Did you forget the information? Or was it something you hadn't learned? Go back and study any shaky areas that the practice tests reveal.

Taking these tests not only helps with your grade, but also aids in combating test anxiety. If you're already used to the test conditions, you're less likely to worry about it, and working through tests until you're scoring well gives you a confidence boost. Go through the practice tests until you feel comfortable, and then you can go into the test knowing that you're ready for it.

Test Tips

On test day, you should be confident, knowing that you've prepared well and are ready to answer the questions. But aside from preparation, there are several test day strategies you can employ to maximize your performance.

First, as stated before, get a good night's sleep the night before the test (and for several nights before that, if possible). Go into the test with a fresh, alert mind rather than staying up late to study.

Try not to change too much about your normal routine on the day of the test. It's important to eat a nutritious breakfast, but if you normally don't eat breakfast at all, consider eating just a protein bar. If you're a coffee drinker, go ahead and have your normal coffee. Just make sure you time it so that the caffeine doesn't wear off right in the middle of your test. Avoid sugary beverages, and drink enough water to stay hydrated but not so much that you need a restroom break 10 minutes into the test. If your test isn't first thing in the morning, consider going for a walk or doing a light workout before the test to get your blood flowing.

Allow yourself enough time to get ready, and leave for the test with plenty of time to spare so you won't have the anxiety of scrambling to arrive in time. Another reason to be early is to select a good seat. It's helpful to sit away from doors and windows, which can be distracting. Find a good seat, get out your supplies, and settle your mind before the test begins.

When the test begins, start by going over the instructions carefully, even if you already know what to expect. Make sure you avoid any careless mistakes by following the directions.

Then begin working through the questions, pacing yourself as you've practiced. If you're not sure on an answer, don't spend too much time on it, and don't let it shake your confidence. Either skip it and come back later, or eliminate as many wrong answers as possible and guess among the remaining ones. Don't dwell on these questions as you continue—put them out of your mind and focus on what lies ahead.

Be sure to read all of the answer choices, even if you're sure the first one is the right answer. Sometimes you'll find a better one if you keep reading. But don't second-guess yourself if you do immediately know the answer. Your gut instinct is usually right. Don't let test anxiety rob you of the information you know.

If you have time at the end of the test (and if the test format allows), go back and review your answers. Be cautious about changing any, since your first instinct tends to be correct, but make sure you didn't misread any of the questions or accidentally mark the wrong answer choice. Look over any you skipped and make an educated guess.

At the end, leave the test feeling confident. You've done your best, so don't waste time worrying about your performance or wishing you could change anything. Instead, celebrate the successful completion of this test. And finally, use this test to learn how to deal with anxiety even better next time.

> **Review Video: 5 Tips to Beat Test Anxiety**
> Visit mometrix.com/academy and enter code: 570656

Important Qualification

Not all anxiety is created equal. If your test anxiety is causing major issues in your life beyond the classroom or testing center, or if you are experiencing troubling physical symptoms related to your anxiety, it may be a sign of a serious physiological or psychological condition. If this sounds like your situation, we strongly encourage you to seek professional help.

Thank You

We at Mometrix would like to extend our heartfelt thanks to you, our friend and patron, for allowing us to play a part in your journey. It is a privilege to serve people from all walks of life who are unified in their commitment to building the best future they can for themselves.

The preparation you devote to these important testing milestones may be the most valuable educational opportunity you have for making a real difference in your life. We encourage you to put your heart into it—that feeling of succeeding, overcoming, and yes, conquering will be well worth the hours you've invested.

We want to hear your story, your struggles and your successes, and if you see any opportunities for us to improve our materials so we can help others even more effectively in the future, please share that with us as well. **The team at Mometrix would be absolutely thrilled to hear from you!** So please, send us an email (support@mometrix.com) and let's stay in touch.

If you'd like some additional help, check out these other resources we offer for your exam:

http://MometrixFlashcards.com/NESINC

Additional Bonus Material

Due to our efforts to try to keep this book to a manageable length, we've created a link that will give you access to all of your additional bonus material.

Please visit http://www.mometrix.com/bonus948/nesinceceri to access the information.